I've wead
What a story!!! I've been there!
It was quite a country!!!.
Mum...

Warriors of Tibet

Warriors of Tibet

The Story of Aten,
and the Khampas' Fight for the
Freedom of their Country

Jamyang Norbu

Wisdom Publications London

First published in 1979 by the Information Office,
Central Tibetan Secretariat, Dharamsala, India

This new edition published in 1986
Wisdom Publications
23 Dering Street
London W1, England

© Tibetan Information Office, Dharamsala 1986

British Library Cataloguing in Publication Data
Aten
    Warriors of Tibet: the story of Aten and the
    Khampas' fight for the freedom of their country.
    1. Khams pa (Tibetan people) – History
    I. Title   II. Norbu, Jamyang
    951'.5   DS731.K5

ISBN 0 86171 050 9

Set in Garamond 10½ on 13 point by Eurasia Press
of Singapore and printed and bound by Eurasia
Press and Biddles of Guildford, Surrey, on 85 gsm
Graphic Text paper supplied by Link Publishing
Papers of West Byfleet, Surrey.

Contents

Preface

Besides the accounts of a few Christian missionaries and English and American consular personnel, very little has been written about Kham or Eastern Tibet. Almost nothing has been recorded of this land during the stormy period it underwent in the nineteen fifties. To understand the Tibetan attitude towards the Chinese and the great revolt in 1959, it is essential to know about Kham. It was from Kham that the revolt began and it was the ferocity and courage of the Khampa warriors that sustained it until the last guerrilla bases in Mustang were destroyed not so many years ago.

This is the account of Aten, a Khampa from Nyarong, one of the largest and most important districts of Eastern Tibet. His experiences are not only typical of what most Khampas had to undergo during that period, but also unusual in that Aten was a trusted accomplice of the Chinese and had been educated in China. After his escape from Tibet in 1960 he came to Dharamsala, where he related his experiences to His Holiness the Dalai Lama. At the insistence of His Holiness, Aten's statement was recorded by the foreign office of the Tibetan Government-in-exile, where for many years it lay in their records.

In 1974 I was persuaded by Mr. Sonam Topgyal, the Secretary of the Information Office, to turn this brief refugee's statement into a book. Soon after, I met Aten and began a series of interviews with him. One of the problems I had to overcome was the Nyarong dialect that Aten spoke, which initially caused me some frustration. Another problem was the reticence with which he answered questions concerning the more intimate and emotional aspects of his experiences. I suppose that no one really cares to resurrect painful memories, but certain Khampas have a tendency to regard any revelation of one's sorrows as a sign of weakness. But otherwise Aten was extremely co-operative. Moreover, he had an amazingly retentive memory and he supplied me with detailed information about his own life and the land and people of Nyarong. (The names of the Chinese officers as given to me by Aten are at best only approximate, due to the combined problems of Tibetan pronunciation of Chinese names and the fact that Chinese officers were usually known by rank and surname only.)

Due to my involvement in a number of political activities, I didn't really begin writing this book until the summer of 1977 when I temporarily put aside my political commitments. The first draft was written in relative peace and comfort thanks to my friend George Burrell, who generously offered me his home and hospitality.

I have attempted as far as possible to make the narrative conform to Aten's character and style of expression. I am not too sure how far I have succeeded in this, but Aten himself seemed satisfied with my rendering of his story and has used my work as a model for a Tibetan version.

I am indebted to my friends Lodi Gyari and Sonam Topgyal for their advice and help. Among many others who aided me with information, I must particularly mention the Nyarong chieftain, Gyari Nima, and his gracious wives Norzin and Dorjee Yudon who regaled me with innumerable tales of their native land.

JAMYANG NORBU
Dharamsala
October, 1979

1 The Early Years

I am an old man now. Age has robbed me of my strength and fate has stolen all that was ever dear to me. From this lofty peak of my old age, I look back towards the memories of my young days, and they still stand before me, vivid and clear as the crystal streams of my land Nyarong. It was a beautiful land, and the lives we led there, though simple and hard, were happy.

Then the Chinese came. At first with soft words and bright silver and later with guns and death. They took away my fields, my animals and my home. They looted, desecrated and burnt the temples and monasteries I worshipped in. Like vermin, they slew my friends, relatives, lamas, and all the people dear to my heart. On a frozen wasteland, thinly covered with wind-swept snow, I left behind me the twisted, bullet-ridden carcasses of my family and my only little daughter.

I was forced to live in the high mountains like an animal, and like a thief to hide by day and to move by night. Hunger and thirst, exhaustion and pain were my constant companions. Bullets ripped and tore through my flesh and muscles. My wounds putrified and rot ate the flesh until my world was a haze of dull pain and the overpowering stench of gangrene. So much sorrow, so much pain and death ... Not only did it prey upon my life and the lives of my countrymen then, but still now it exists and feeds on my poor people back in Tibet. They live in despair night and day, in a country that has become an endless nightmare. Everything has been taken away from them: their faith, their dignity, their manhood and their freedom ... except perhaps, the freedom to starve, to slave and to die. Yes, I remember it all. Pain and bitterness have etched every moment and event forever into my mind. As I recall each incident, it is as vivid and real as every shining bead of the rosary I hold in my old hands now.

The first memories I have are of myself as a little boy running on the green meadows surrounding Dhunkhug, my village. When summer came the meadows were carpeted with a brilliant mosaic of primulas, edelweiss, daisies and hundreds of other wild flowers. We would take off our boots and run among the flowers, feeling their freshness and life beneath our bare feet. We used to play on the sides of the green hills all day long, making garlands and crowns of wild flowers. We would lie down and bask in the sweet, heady scent of the flowers, watching clouds of various shapes drifting in the turquoise sky.

Far to the north, where the sky touched the horizon, towered the great mountain Khawa Lo Ring, which means the Heights of Eternal Snow. Three distinct peaks rose jaggedly into the heavens, the tallest bearing a mantle of pristine snow throughout the year. The guardian spirit of this mountain was known as Eternal Snow, and was reputed to be a minister at the court of Nyenchen Thanglha, the mighty spirit ruler of the Trans-Himalayan range. The hills around our village were not so high and were only covered in snow in winter. They ran roughly in an east-west direction and the southern slopes were all meadow, dotted with small groves of trees. We called them *nyimo* (sunny). The northern slopes which received little sunlight were called *se* (cool) and were covered with thick dark forests.

The forests were alive with animals: deer of many kinds, the bucks usually living alone, while the females and their fawns grazed in small herds; monkeys chattered and screamed from the trees, hurling abuse at the leopards that stalked them; bears snuffled about for roots, plants and insects while their bigger cousin, the giant brown bear, hunted for more substantial fare. I remember another animal we called the *sha gya*. It was like a small deer with a pure white back. There were also lynx, foxes, jackals and occasionally a solitary tiger.

On the southern side of the hills were hares that we called *rigung* and Pika mouse-hares (*abras*). We used to call the little *abra* the great hermit because of its serious countenance and its habit of living in solitude. In these meadows roamed small herds of shy dainty Tibetan gazelles, and occasionally a musk deer could also be seen. The musk deer is a delicate creature that has, instead of horns, a set of long tusk-like canines which it uses in territorial combat and for defence. These deer were much prized for a certain gland in their bodies that had medicinal properties.

Higher up the rocky slopes where there was little or no vegetation, wandered large herds of Blue Sheep and the sure-footed *nyen*, which had large horns that curled in exquisite spirals. These heights were also the domain of the snow leopard. Its soft grey to pure white coat starred with pale rosettes blended perfectly with the terrain of snow and rocks.

I was born in 1915, the Year of the Female Wood Hare, and was named Rapten Dorje, the Steadfast Thunderbolt, but I was generally called Aten. It was the custom in my land to give every man a diminutive name of two syllables: the first syllable always being the vowel AH of the Tibetan alphabet. In its religious context, AH is the root, the primordial sound. Thus people were generally known as Aten, Aben, Agon and so on, rather than by their real names. My family name was Daghya Tsang.

When I was about twelve, an age when boys could and were made to work, I used to take my family's sheep and yaks to graze in the meadows. There would be other boys from the village, and we used to sit on the hillside all day long, playing our flutes and wrestling or hitting distant rocks with our slings. The slings were woven of yak-hair and had a tuft of wool at the end that caused a noise like a pistol-shot when the projectile was released. I remember the sling my mother made for me. It was woven from black and white yak-hair and had the auspicious design of the Nine Eyes for warding off evil spirits and ghosts. These slings were by no means play things. They were an effective defence against bold jackals, wolves and Lammergeyer eagles that had a partiality for solitary lambs. For ammunition, we used pebbles the size of our fists, and most of the boys were extremely accurate. Many could shatter a yak horn at a hundred paces.

We used to bring our midday meals from the village in woollen bags, which most of the time would be brown bread baked in hot ashes, or roasted barley meal (*tsampa*). With this we might have a hunk of boiled mutton, sausages, or a strip or two of beef. This simple meal was usually garnished with pickled radishes and washed down with a bowl or two of *chang*, effervescent barley-ale. The *chang* was usually watered down for the children. In the evening we drove our animals back to the village. We would adorn ourselves and the animals with garlands of wild flowers — and a most colourful and happy procession would wend its way home.

The village of Dhunkhug was a humble one, consisting of about six families. All these families were large and it was normal for a family to have fifteen to twenty members. Our house, built in the customary manner, was three stories high and made of stone. Sometimes houses were also built from rammed earth — it all depended on the availability of building materials in the locality. Our animals were sheltered on the ground floor within the walled courtyard. Above that were the store-rooms where our grain, fodder, meat and other provisions were kept. The second floor had bedrooms and a big kitchen, which was the natural centre for family life. It was a warm place, full of good smells, which to my young mind radiated a great sense of security and satisfaction. I used to sit in the kitchen for hours on end, watching the flames dancing in the big hearth, while my mother bustled about preparing the evening meal.

Supper was the main meal of the day and the most enjoyable. Then the whole family came together, and seated on ottomans behind low tables discussed the events of the day.

Mostly, we ate various kinds of stews made from turnips, potatoes and chunks of yak meat or mutton. Sometimes we had soup with dumplings, and if we were lucky my mother would prepare a special dessert of *droma* cooked in butter. The *droma* is a tiny cluster of roots found in the hills, usually in spring and autumn. These roots are sweet and have a delicious flavour. Armed with baskets and bags, digging sticks and old knives, we used to scour the hillsides in search of this delicacy. In spring the *droma* is sweetest, whereas in autumn it is much bigger in size. It is dried in the sun and stored for use on festive occasions such as the New Year. We ate from wooden bowls manufactured by a community of turners living around Chako Dzong, the Iron Castle, in the east. Our spoons were generally made from silver or brass. Chopsticks, introduced by the Chinese, were a novelty then and were used by the nobility in Lhasa or by rich merchants.

The whole family ate together, including the servants, the hired hands and any passing pilgrim or trader. Hospitality was a deeply ingrained custom. Even the meanest homes would never turn away a traveller who sought food and shelter. I do not mean to imply that we were extraordinarily good people. The traveller more than paid for his food and shelter with fresh news of Lhasa and distant lands. There were accounts of feuds, wars and intrigues; tales of gods, saints and miracles; perhaps a description of his journey — mountains ruled by strange spirits, secret lakes where mysterious visions could be seen, storms, avalanches and encounters with fierce bandits, wild savages and malicious ghosts.

After dinner, when the tables were cleared, father would pull out his pipe and smoke. He had a beautiful pipe, as long as his arm, embossed with silver. By the light of two butter lamps he would talk about the crops, the animals or the events of the day, pausing now and then to down copious drafts of barley-ale. I can see him now — a tall, lanky man, easily over six feet tall. He had fine aquiline features and deep penetrating eyes. His hair was unusual for it was completely white, and had been that way since his youth. His name was Gonpo

Tsewang, but he was generally known as Ahgon. He was born in 1880, the Male Iron Dragon Year, and was liked and respected by most people for his astuteness and honesty, and also because his father had served the Tibetan Government loyally and had been awarded with a rank and an official seal. In his teens, my father had been to Lhasa as a servant of a Government monk official, Dhakpa Kalden. He studied there for many years and eventually returned to Nyarong, our province, as a scholar of sorts. He had beautiful handwriting, and when it came to drafting official missives and legal documents, he was without equal.

By tribal rank he was the Arrow Chief — head of our sub-tribe, Wuya. It consisted of ten villages and their surrounding land — about a hundred families. The province of Nyarong itself was divided into four tribes called the Seat of a Thousand which implied that, theoretically, each tribe consisted of about a thousand families. Every tribe was divided into sub-tribes. One tribe usually consisted of ten to fifteen sub-tribes. We belonged to the tribe of Wulu.

Except for the monasteries there were no regular schools in Nyarong. So my father took it into his own hands to educate me and my brothers. As was the custom in Tibet, he first taught us an invocation to the sublime deity of wisdom, Jampelyang (Manjushri), whose sacred mantra OM AH RA PA TSA NA DHI we had to repeat many times. Starting on wooden slates we were taught to write the sacred alphabet and later to read religious texts and works on grammar and poetry. We also learned the history of Tibet and the maxims and wise sayings of our people:

> Those with little learning are proud:
> The truly wise are humble.
> The babbling brooks are noisy,
> But the ocean is quiet.

But most of all my father wanted us to be well-mannered and

cultured, and he would constantly quote this proverb to us:

> Dogs and dragons must growl,
> Tea and beer must be sustaining,
> Men and horses must have breeding.

He married my mother when he was twenty-five. My mother, Dorje Lhachee, was the daughter of a nomad chieftain, Wendo Tsang. She was a tall and handsome woman, strong and hard-working. She was independent by nature, and she ran the household with a firm but gentle hand. I remember, when I was very small, tagging along behind her as she went about her household duties: cleaning the rooms, scouring the copper utensils in the kitchen until they shone like gold, and making tea. Tibetan tea is made with special tea leaves from China mixed with butter and a pinch of soda and salt. I can remember a song describing the recipe.

> One, the best tea from China,
> Two, the pure *dre** butter of Tibet,
> Three, the white salt from the northern plains,
> All three from different places,
> All meeting in the copper pot.
> Yet, how the tea is brewed
> Is up to you, O Tea maker.

The mixture was boiled and churned in a long wooden cylinder, which was fitted with a plunger. When the plunger was driven up and down, it made gurgling and belching sounds which used to delight my childish mind. I would roll about with laughter at the rude and funny noises made by the tea churn.

But, best of all, I liked going with my mother to our family shrine-room, on the third floor of our house. The shrine-room always used to fascinate me — the soft smell of incense,

---

*dre — female yak. Tibetans use the term yak only for the male animal.

the perfect neatness and the beautifully polished wooden floor that reflected the flickering flames of the sacred lamps and the many holy images they illuminated. The centre-piece of our shrine was a gilded image of Lord Buddha. To his right was an image of Padma Sambhava or Guru Rinpoche, the great Indian saint and tantric master who turned the Wheel of the Law in Tibet, despite the active opposition of many demons and gods. He is depicted as a strong, aggressive person with dark, piercing eyes and a black moustache curling over his upper lip. There was also a beautiful silver and gold image of Chenrezig, the sublime embodiment of mercy and the patron deity of all Tibet. His Holiness the Dalai Lama is a manifestation of this deity and is thus revered, not only by our people, but by many Chinese Buddhists, Mongols and also, I have heard, by other people in more distant lands. Later on, I managed to acquire a hand-tinted photograph of the Thirteenth Dalai Lama, Thubten Gyatso, which, in a silver frame, took the prominent place in our shrine-room.

All Tibetans have a great love and reverence for this short, unassuming, pock-marked monk who became the ruler of Tibet and died of over-work, striving to free his ancient nation and better the lot of his beloved subjects. The connection of every Tibetan with the Dalai Lama is a deep and inexpressible thing. To us, the Dalai Lama symbolises the whole of Tibet: the beauty of the land, the purity of its rivers and lakes, the sanctity of its skies, the solidity of its mountains, and the strength of its people. But even more, he is the living embodiment of the eternal principles of Buddhism, and also the epitome of what every Tibetan, from the most debauched harlot in Lhasa to the saintly ascetic, is striving and longing for — freedom, the total freedom of Nirvana.

I remember the simple prayers and invocations my mother taught me as a small child, and which, with closed eyes and palms folded together, I used to recite in our shrine-room. If I begged hard enough and promised to be careful, my mother would lift me up and let me light the offering lamps. Holding my breath eagerly, and with a burning taper in my hand, I would carefully light the fresh lamps filled with good butter. When the wicks caught alight, I would see seven golden flames dancing upside down in the seven silver bowls full of water.*

My mother was a very religious woman. When she worked, she constantly murmured prayers, and she gave generously to every beggar and pilgrim who came to our door. I remember those cold, dark winter nights when wolves howled mournfully in the snow. I would wake up in great fear and, crying, would rush to my mother's bed. It was considered to be very unlucky to hear a wolf's howl and my mother would solemnly say, "throw dust in the wolf's mouth and strike a peg in his eye." This incantation was supposed to ward off bad luck. She would then hold me close to her under the blankets and softly croon an old folk song:

> On the tall snowy peaks,
> The little lion cub is playing.
> Oh you mountains, please be gentle,
> Till the cub has grown his mane.

I had two brothers and a sister. My sister, who was three years older than me, decided to lead a religious life and became a nun. Her name was Dechen Lhamo. She lived with my old aunt, who was also a nun, in a distant hermitage. On occasion they would visit us and always bring something nice for me and my brothers. Sometimes it would be molasses candy or perhaps dried fruit. They would also bring dried cheese, which was my favourite delicacy. This cheese is made in small cubes strung together in loops. The cubes are as hard as rocks and equally tough to chew, but they are nutritious and have a sweet and pungent flavour. They are a favourite

---

*All Tibetans make offerings of water to the Buddha and other deities. This custom originated from the Indian pandit, Atisha, who when questioned by his Tibetan disciples on what manner of offerings they should make to the Buddha, replied that the water of Tibet was so pure and sweet it would be an ideal offering. The offering of plain water also denotes the equality of all devotees, regardless of position or wealth.

with children and with travellers, who break the monotony of
their journeys by chewing them for hours on end. Old people
liked this dried cheese, believing quite rightly that it would
exercise their gums and help keep their teeth intact.

My younger brother, Pema Namgyal, whom we affec-
tionately called Aben, also became a monk when he was very
young and was recognised as a *tulku*, that is, an incarnation
of some saint, ascetic or a great lama. He was a delicate boy,
beautiful and very intelligent, and it did not surprise us when
he was declared the reincarnation of the great Chandi Rinpoche. I was very fond of him and we were always as thick as
thieves, especially when we were up to some mischief. It was
a lonely day for me when a procession of monks took him
away to the monastery of Chandi, the Iron Knot, high up
on a plateau, about three hours ride from my village. There he
was to begin his education and training for his propitious
vocation. Although it was sad to see him go, I rather envied
him.

We children used to find a great sense of romance in our
religion. Undoubtedly, the stories of great saints like Milarepa
and the sage Pema Dadhul of Nyarong strongly impressed
themselves on our adolescent minds. It was quite understand-
able. The stories of these men were nearly all exciting and
adventurous — ascetics pitting themselves against evil sorcerers and demoniacal forces, silently meditating in inaccessible
mountain reaches, and by miraculous means projecting themselves into strange worlds and the extremities of the universe.
Some of the tales were very humorous and many were poi-
gnant. The heroes of these stories were intensely real, wise
and compassionate, and so implacably strong that no child
could ever help but hero-worship them. Many men renounced their worldly possessions and took to a life of con-
templation and religious striving. Even children, on occasion,
ran away from home in emulation of their saintly heroes.

Stories of battles and ambushes, valour and daring were
also immensely popular in Eastern Tibet. The best known
and most violent of these were the *Epics of Gesar*. These epics

are in verse and were sung by roving bards. Their origin is unknown. The verses relate the adventures of Prince Gesar of the Kingdom of Ling, and the many wars and battles he waged with neighbouring tribes and kingdoms. He gathered together a host of mighty warriors — the formidable Dabhla, fierce Shenba, brave Dherma and the exasperating trickster Uncle Trodung, who both helped and hindered Gesar with his numerous and ingenious pranks.

These epics abound with the non-human characters like gods, fierce titans, demons and imps that Gesar had to contend with. There are also beautiful maidens to be rescued and seduced, flying steeds and magical swords that sang warnings when the enemy was near.

Gesar and his warriors never died, and even now, after nearly one thousand three hundred years, travellers riding across the Great Northern Plains have seen them. If you happened to be crossing some isolated stretch of grassland and encountered a noble encampment surrounded by magnificent steeds and gigantic yaks, and if you saw a princely figure flanked by armed stalwarts in glittering suits of armour, you would, with some trepidation, realise that this was *him*. And you would judiciously give the place a wide berth, knowing that heroes are quick to anger and resent intrusion.

I would listen to these stories for hours on end, and a great and fierce longing used to rise in my heart. Indeed, there is a Tibetan proverb that says:

> The stories of Milarepa may make
> A rich man's son into a saint.
> But the Epics of Gesar will surely
> Impale the beggar boy on a sword.

One great lover of the Epics was my elder brother Wangchen, who was as fearless as he was handsome. He was a reckless and skilled rider and the downfall of every village maiden. I worshipped him when I was a boy, and he good-naturedly allowed me to tag along with him whenever he rode off on some escapade.

I had another companion who was my own age. His name was Nyima and he was an orphan who lived and worked for us. He was a brave and loyal boy, and we were great friends. Much later, when the land was torn with war and strife, we battled together against the enemy ... but I go too far ahead in my tale ... Let me return to the days when we were boys and told each other tales of battles, ghosts and witches while we were safely and warmly tucked away in our thick quilts and blankets. When the weather was fine, we would sleep on the roof tops and trade stories as we watched the effulgent stars glittering in the dark, endless skies of Nyarong. Slowly, the conversation would dwindle to a murmur, and we would fall asleep.

2 Heritage of Freedom

A strong hand shook me by the shoulders, waking me from
deep sleep.

"Wake up Aten, we have to go soon."

Grumbling and cursing softly, I rolled over in my blankets
to go back to sleep. Again the hand shook me urgently.

"Get up quick. Father is having breakfast. We have to leave
for the *dzong** soon."

Suddenly I remembered and woke up with a start. It was
my elder brother Wangchen, a wide grin breaking over his
handsome features. "You sleep like a pig, Aten. I thought
you would never wake up." He walked over to the door.
"Hurry up and get dressed, or you won't have time to eat."

I got up and looked out of the window. It was still dark but
my brother had left a small lamp behind. I quickly washed
and put on my best clothes, which I had taken out of my
leather-bound box and laid out the previous night. I put on a
clean tussore-silk shirt with a high collar, a brown brocade
waist-coat, and tucked the ends of my baggy trousers into my
black felt boots. Over all this I put on my voluminous robe,
hitched up just below my knees and secured around the waist
with a long red silk belt. The robe was lined with lambskin
and trimmed with sable. Tying my dagger at my side and
picking up my fox-skin cap, I hastened to the kitchen. Of
course, I never wore these clothes normally. They were reserved for festivals like the New Year. But today was a very
special day.

* Castle or fortress, generally the district headquarters.

Ever since my birth, Nyarong and the major portion of Eastern Tibet, or Kham, had been conquered and occupied by the Chinese Nationalist Army. Although they claimed to act under the directives of the Nationalist Government, they were more or less an independent army under the ruthless leadership of the war lord, Liu Wu Hen. Prior to the Nationalists, we had been under the occupation of Imperial Manchu troops for eight years.

The Chinese soldiers, though well armed with modern rifles, were on the whole a poor and indifferent lot. Many of them were opium addicts, whose officers used them as coolies to transport opium to China, or otherwise made them work in the goldfields of Thau and Drango. The officers were rapacious and brutal with a cool indifference towards their duties. When the commanding officer of a garrison received the soldiers' pay-roll, he took a percentage of it as his cut, and then passed it on to the next officer below him, who did the same. By the time the money got through the ranks, there was very little left to be distributed to the common soldier. Undoubtedly, this sort of skullduggery took place even in the higher ranks of generals and politicians. This attitude of the Nationalists was in many ways a boon to us, and we bought a measure of freedom with bribes and favours. Anyhow, their general inefficiency and also a lurking fear of insurrection made them leave us pretty much alone. But they had to have their "presents," and on occasion they could be very cruel.

But in the spring of 1931, the Female Iron Sheep Year, the monastery of Dhargay in Tri Hor, north of Nyarong, revolted against its Chinese overlords. Over the years, the monks had secretly acquired a motley but large collection of arms, which they proceeded to use with vigour. The Chinese rushed in soldiers to quell the rebellion, and fighting broke out in that area. The monastery was besieged, and in desperation the monks appealed to the Tibetan Government in Lhasa for help. The cabinet responded immediately and commenced hostilities with China. The gods were with us, and after several months of intense fighting, the Chinese soldiers were driven back. Two regiments under the command of General Sonam Wangdu of the noble house of Khemey entered Nyarong. After many battles with the Chinese army, they captured the Castle of the Female Dragon, along with the garrison and the Chinese commander, General Tang, whom the people of Nyarong called Old Pot Head, in reference to his baldness. This was our momentous day. Chieftains from all over our province were gathering at the Castle to pay their respects to the victorious Tibetan General.

I quickly had my breakfast and rushed down to the court-yard where my father and brother were waiting. I saddled my pony and we rode out of the courtyard. At the gate, our huge black mastiff, Rabshug — Great Strength — growled menacingly at the end of his thick chain. Recognizing us, he ambled back to his kennel to sleep.

As we rode out, the first lights of dawn glowed on the horizon. Soon, streaks of sunlight darted from the breaks in the eastern hills, lighting up the peaks of the dark mountains opposite. The sun rose. The air was cold and invigorating. I breathed in deeply through my nose and felt the stinging sharpness of the cold air. Tears of pain and pleasure rolled down my cheeks, and I sang an old travelling song.

> The noble steed is like the precious Jewel,
> The golden saddle is like the Jewel Ornament
> When the golden bridle is put on his head ... then
>   we must go.
> Do not whip the noble steed, but seek refuge in
>   the Lama.
> The young tiger man is like the Precious Jewel,
> The three weapons are like the Jewel Ornament
> When he wears his fox-skin cap ... then we must
>   go.
> Do not fall in an ambush, but seek refuge in the
>   Lama.

My father and brother laughed aloud and joined me in my song. They were also dressed in their best. My brother's robe was trimmed with leopard skin and he looked extremely pleased with himself. We have a proverb that says: "As friends we like the old, as clothes we like the new."

We were all armed with rifles, swords and our usual daggers. My father also had a Mauser pistol with a wooden holster and stock combination. His sword was our prized family heirloom and was famous. It was called Eternal Starlight. This blade had abruptly ended many a life, and was considered to have magical powers. It was a priceless treasure and had been in our family since time immemorial. With my Russian rifle and sword, and draped with bandoliers of ammunition, I felt strong and truculent. Woe betide any bandit or miserable Chinaman that crossed my path. I was a man now — I was sixteen years old.

We followed the little stream that flowed past our village, and entering a small grove of trees we gently descended the hillside towards the valley of the River Nya Chu, the Water of the Hollows. We proceeded for over an hour, until the roar of the big river told us that we were approaching. By this time we were down in the broad valley and we followed the river up north to our destination — the great Castle of the Female Dragon, which had been the headquarters of our province since the beginning of the history of Nyarong.

According to my father, the people of Nyarong and perhaps even the whole of Kham, were the descendants of the garrisons posted on the frontiers by the great Emperor of Tibet, Trisong Deu Tsen, who had also conquered Northern China in the eighth century. At that time, the Empire of Tibet stretched all the way east from Northern China, to the west, bordering the Empire of the Caliph of Baghdad.

When the Empire disintegrated under the improvident rule of the apostate Lang Darma, Nyarong, like many other provinces of Tibet, drifted into oblivion and broke up into petty warring tribes. After about four hundred years of anarchy, Tibet was finally reunited by the new Sakya dynasty.

Yet there was no firm ruler in Nyarong, and it was rife with banditry and internecine feuds. Despite the general lawlessness, the people clung tenaciously to their old customs and beliefs. We never changed our religion and our language, and the rulers of Tibet were, in our hearts, our rulers. With the coming of the Dalai Lamas, this loyalty was permanently ensured.

Then, in the early nineteenth century, there rose a man in Nyarong who, through sheer ability and ruthlessness, united the whole of Eastern Tibet, drove the Chinese back to the borders of the ancient emperors and made the Manchu Emperor of China quiver in his satin shoes. His name was Gonpo Namgyal. He was a stout man with a large, impressive head, and his face was always flushed. He had lost one eye in battle, and the remaining one protruded violently from its socket, like the eye of a fish. He was a blunt man who wasted no words, and demanded that others do likewise. He was brave to the point of recklessness and extravagantly generous, but he was totally ruthless to his enemies. Not much is known of his early days, except that he was the chief of some small tribe. But around the year of the Female Wood Sheep (1835), his fame began to spread. He subjugated neighbouring tribes, and apparently not satisfied, began to add whole clans to his list of conquests. After a few years, all Nyarong was his. He then systematically began a rapid conquest of the provinces of Eastern Tibet. His armies overran Drango, Tri Hor, Masuer and Khongbar. He defeated and deposed the kings of Bheru and Chala, right on the Chinese frontier. He then further added the lands of Geshe, Trosha, Batang, Lithang, Chatring, Minya, Gyathong, Derge, Lingtsang, Lhatog and Nadre Shoksum to his list of conquests. The twenty-four chieftains of Gaba were ground into submission, and finally he conquered the vast northern expanse of Golok, the land of the legendary bandit tribes. He failed only to conquer the province of Amdo, the extreme northern extent of Tibet. Otherwise he had taken back and united every inch of land within the frontiers established by the ancient Tibetan emperors. His dominion was commonly known as the Eighty thousand families of Nyarong.

He then proceeded to consolidate his gains. He threw out all the old chieftains and kings of his conquered lands and appointed new chieftains that were loyal to him. To ensure the end of powerful and hostile coalitions, and the destruction, once and for all, of petty kings and chieftains, he compelled rich families to marry their sons and daughters into poor families. He built a splendid palace, eight stories high, at the Hill of Meadows, a day's ride from the Female Dragon Castle.

His laws were harsh, but swift and just — and except for his constant wars, the people were generally contented. Gonpo Namgyal was not an exceptionally religious man, but he was a firm believer and a devout supplicant of the fierce deity Gonpo, his namesake. Each year he held a great prayer meeting of three thousand monks to invoke this deity. Otherwise his approach to religious matters was rough and ready. To ensure the authenticity of lamas and saints, he demanded that they perform miracles on the spot for him.

As Gonpo Namgyal began to cast his single ambitious eye upon new and further conquests, the Manchu Emperor of China became enraged. This barbarous upstart, this petty chief of some insignificant Tibetan tribes, had in a few strokes deprived the Celestial Empire of the fruits of centuries of painful conquests and brain-racking intrigues. Something had to be done. The Celestial Empire could not, at this juncture, afford to expend its energies and resources on starting a long and expensive war with the western barbarians.

The Amban, the Manchurian representative in Lhasa, began to drop unsettling rumours into the ears of the Tibetan Government. The Twelfth Dalai Lama was still a minor, and the regent was convinced that Gonpo Namgyal was a rebel. Frightening stories began to spread in the Holy City. One of the rumours circulating was that Gonpo Namgyal had sworn to ransack Lhasa and carry off as a trophy the famed image of the Jowo, Buddha Sakyamuni, from the Great Cathedral. In vain, Gonpo Namgyal sent couriers to plead his innocence and loyalty.

Finally, the Tibetan Government decided to make the first move. An army under the Minister Tsewang Dorje Phulu and Trimon Chime Dorje was hastily despatched to Eastern Tibet. Fighting broke out, and this civil war carried on indecisively for two years. Finally, Gonpo Namgyal, tired of this internecine fighting, declared his intentions for a truce.

In 1865, the year of the Wood Ox, the Tibetan Commanders and Gonpo Namgyal met. Gonpo Namgyal declared he had always been loyal to the Dalai Lama, and had no intention of ever betraying him. He further stated that his only enemy was China, and all he had ever done was to re-conquer lands that the Chinese had torn away from Tibet. He said he did not want to fight any more, and to prove his innocence declared his willingness to swear fealty to the Tibetan Government. He only demanded that Trimon Chime Dorje, the Tibetan Commander, should swear never to betray him. According to a custom of Nyarong, both parties pledged to "give each other their merits and bear each other's sins." Before an image of the fierce Gonpo, each lit a butter lamp, made his pledge and swore his oaths. But matters were not to end so easily. Gonpo Namgyal was murdered when he least expected it, and his palace burned down. Trimon had triumphed.

Even now in Nyarong, when we refer to an act of treachery or perjury, we call it The Oath of Trimon. However, Gonpo Namgyal's efforts were not entirely in vain, for Eastern Tibet was reunited with the rest of Tibet. For about forty years we were free. Nyarong annually paid taxes of 120 *sangs* of gold and 2700 *sangs* of silver to the central Government, as well as a large amount of bear gall and wooden bowls and plates. The beautifully crafted wooden bowls of Nyarong even graced the tables of the Potala Palace.

Nevertheless, the Tibetan Government could not retain Gonpo Namgyal's conquests. China continued to plan the capture of Tibet, and in 1880, the Male Dragon Year, the reconstituted kings of Chala and Nadre Shoksum, the provinces on the frontier, allied themselves with China.

In 1896, the Male Fire Monkey Year, the Manchu Emperor sent his army to take over the frontiers, but due to many difficulties, it was only in 1903, the Female Water Hare Year, that the Chinese army under General Chao Er Feng invaded Lithang and Batang from the south. Butcher Feng, as we Tibetans called him, was a man of immense cruelty. He burned the great monastery of Batang to the ground, and made his soldiers use the scriptures to re-sole their shoes. Many Tibetans were executed by decapitation or by another typically Chinese method, mass burial while still alive. Little by little, the frontiers began to fall and gradually the whole of Eastern Tibet was occupied by the Chinese. For the first time in history, Nyarong was conquered by China. The Manchu dynasty fell and was later replaced by the Nationalist Government. This made no difference to us — we were still the chattels of alien conquerors.

But on this day, after thirty long years of living under the hated Chinese, we were again part of our land, Tibet. And I was to be a living witness of this momentous occasion.

I emerged from my thoughts and realised that we had been travelling down the banks of the river for nearly two hours. My father and brother had spurred on their horses and were galloping ahead of me. I dug my heels into the flanks of my horse and raced after them. As I turned the last bend in the river I saw the Castle of the Female Dragon. It was a huge, imposing structure, built of dark granite. The thick walls were pierced with rows of loopholes for the defenders to shoot through, but without artillery of some kind it would have been impossible to break through those massive walls. The castle had been given its peculiar name as it had been built at the end of a long sinewy ridge that descended towards the river, the castle itself being fancifully likened to the head of the dragon drinking from the river. This structure was built during the Sakya dynasty around the thirteenth century. There was a busy little town outside the castle and people from many villages and nomad encampments came here to buy and sell.

I was surprised to see the ancient Lion Standard of Tibet flying proudly from the top of the highest parapet of the castle. I shouted and waved to my father, pointing it out to him. He and my brother saw it and cheered loudly.

We entered the market place, which was busier than I had ever seen it. There were chieftains with their families and retainers, all dressed in brilliant furs and brocades and armed to the hilt. Farmers, nomads, monks, traders and hundreds of others thronged the streets, brushing shoulders with the soldiers of the newly arrived Tibetan army. The soldiers looked tough and were wearing brown or black robes of homespun wool. Most of them wore thick silk and tussore turbans to protect them from sword cuts, others had on fox pelt caps and a few of them sported broad-brimmed felt hats. Although they had no common uniform, they were well organised and disciplined, and they all carried the regulation Lee Metford rifle.

Some of the soldiers were drinking chang in the taverns and talking with the local people. They were undoubtedly narrating highlights of recent battles or proclaiming the cowardice of the Chinese soldiers. The stalls were more numerous than ever and piled high with all sorts of goods and luxuries. Vendors were selling meat, dried fruit, loops of dried cheese and pots of pickled radishes. There were booths overflowing with copper utensils and agricultural implements, stands with rolls of cotton textiles, calico, shantung, brocade and expensive silks. Humbler shops sold homespun wools, yak-hair ropes, blankets and squares of felt. Some merchants retailed brick tea from China under various brand-names: Flaming Jewel, The Wheel and Double Thunderbolt. There were shops displaying beautifully chased saddles, bridles, reins, knives and swords, and most importantly, rifles and ammunition.

I looked at the market place and thought of the Chinese soldiers who had marched through it recently. Then I remembered a brutal incident which had taken place in this square four years earlier, and my heart was filled with sadness.

I had ridden down from my village to deliver a message to one of my father's merchant friends. My errand completed, I was preparing to leave for home, when I heard a great commotion from the market square. I went over to see what was going on. The place was crowded with people, except for the centre of the square, which was quite empty but for a few scruffy Chinese soldiers carrying rifles with fixed bayonets. Rising from the hard-packed earth, was a large wooden cross.

As I was small, I had managed to squeeze through the crowded bodies and push myself to the front. I had no idea why this unusually large crowd had collected here, or why the soldiers had the cross. I listened to the people jabbering over my head:

"What will they do to him? Something bad, I reckon ..."

"But he didn't do anything ..."

"Did you see what happened?"

"... a poor mule driver, the Lord Buddha have mercy on him ..."

"... *om mani padme hum* ... *om mani padme hum* ..."

"It was at the bridge, the Chinese officer had a pistol ..."

"The carrion eaters are always making trouble for us ..."

From what I could gather, a mule train crossing the bridge had inadvertently blocked the passage of a young Chinese officer, a captain. The young captain, enraged at this affront to his dignity, had proceeded to empty the magazine of his pistol into the unfortunate bodies of the mules. The Tibetan muleteer had angrily remonstrated with him, and had undoubtedly cursed him in the strongest of terms. The officer had instructed his soldiers to beat up the muleteer. The captain had then decided to make a spectacle of this insolent Tibetan in the town square, his dignity as yet unrestored by the beating.

A sudden silence fell over the crowd when the muleteer was dragged to the centre of the square. His face was bloated and

misshapen by the punishment he had received, and his back
and arms were a mass of horrible weals and bruises. There
was blood all over him, caked in dirty brown patches. He
could not walk, and one of his legs trailed behind him in an
awkward and unnatural way. I figured they had broken it.

The soldiers dragged him to the cross, which was about
eight feet high, and propped him up against it. Two soldiers
climbed on a bench and pulled his arms upwards, lashing
them against the cross. They tied his fingers tightly at the
upper joints with raw hide, so he could not bend or move
them. Then the soldiers proceeded to insert long bamboo
slivers down between his fingers and nails. They put in six
long slivers, leaving only his thumbs and little fingers free.
Each bamboo sliver was pushed down as far as it would go.
One sliver was pushed in too hard and its razor sharp tip
pierced through the base of his nail.

The muleteer screamed with pain. A low murmur rose
from the crowd and some sobbed aloud. Nearly everyone
was praying in low voices. The soldiers were laughing and
congratulating their captain. They gathered around him
appreciatively, as if thanking him for the entertainment. But
the captain had not yet finished. From his shirt pocket he
pulled out a bundle of small Nationalist Chinese paper flags.
He attached a flag to the end of each long bamboo splint. The
soldiers were now helpless with laughter. They folded their
arms around their sides, rocking back and forth, trying to
catch their breath, while tears rolled down their cheeks. The
captain jauntily stepped down from the bench and, arms
akimbo, paused to admire his handiwork. A little breeze blew
up and the red paper flags fluttered gaily. A low painful howl
came from the battered and shapeless mouth of the victim.

I could not stand any more and I think I must have
screamed. Many people looked towards me. Frantically, I
pushed my way through the crowd and ran in terror from the
place. I managed to reach my horse, and I galloped home.
When I arrived at Dhunkhug, I was sick and hysterical with

fear. I wept inconsolably in my mother's lap for hours. Someone rushed to get my father and he came in from the fields. I was put to bed and my father and mother were constantly beside me. For many days, I was delirious. But slowly the incident faded from my mind and strength returned to my body.

I later learned that the Chinese soldiers had kept the man in the market square for three days — and as the valley was quite windy, the poor man had been in continuous and terrible pain. After three days, the novelty of this gruesome entertainment had begun to pall, so the soldiers cut off his head and stuck it on a pole near the bridge; no doubt, to serve as a warning to all proud and recalcitrant Tibetans.

My father had special services conducted for the benefit of the muleteer, at the nearby monastery of Chandi. As I was only twelve when I witnessed this terrible incident, it left a strong impression on my mind. I dreamt about it many times, even as an adult. This was my first encounter with Chinese brutality.

I shook off this unpleasant reverie when I realised that my father had stopped his conversation with his friends and was looking at me intently, as if he understood the reasons for my sadness. I silently said a prayer for the better rebirth of the muleteer and went over to join my father. With my father and brother were old friends of the family and some of our many relatives. They all greeted me, and my father proudly began recounting my amazing prowess with the Russian rifle which he had given me the year before. The conversation then drifted to the topic of guns and marksmanship.

In a land as lawless and uncertain as ours, a rifle was an essential part of a man's life. This was due to the fear of bandits, who were bold and numerous, but also because of the prevalence of interminable and bloody feuds. Families fought against families, tribes against tribes, often for reasons that were so buried in the past that even the protagonists were not very sure of what they were fighting about. Lamas and monasteries would strive to patch up matters between belligerent parties, and they often succeeded. But no sooner was one feud resolved than another would flare up in a different part of the country. Our people were like that — they just couldn't resist a good fight. There is an old saying that gives a fair idea of how the people of Nyarong (and other parts of Eastern Tibet) behaved:

> A blow on the nose of a hated enemy,
> Is surely more satisfying,
> Than listening to the advice
> Of benevolent parties.

As most of our people were brave and religious there were practically no instances of cruelty or torture such as the Chinese used to practise. A man was shot clean or cut down by a sword in battle. Nevertheless, it was totally deplorable, and sad for the women and children. It gave the Chinese a great advantage in our country. My father was a peaceful man and totally against this sort of thing. His religious education and his stay in Central Tibet (where law and order prevailed) had impressed him with the need for a more secure future for Nyarong. In his zeal for peace, he had even forsworn shooting game. He so impressed me with his convictions that I too, later in life, gave up hunting. Nevertheless, he still loved a good rifle, and his eyes would gleam with pleasure when he handled an unusually fine Czech weapon.

But today the conversation on guns became languid and talk returned to the subject of the amazing success of the Tibetan army and our own great fortune. Some of our people had been with the army as guides and had also fought side by side with the Tibetan soldiers ... stories flew thick and fast.

After a while, we all passed through the massive gates of the great castle and gathered in the large courtyard. The four chieftains, rulers of the four great tribes of Nyarong, were there: Gyari Tsang of Nyatoe (Upper Nyarong); Gyongba Tsang of Nyame (Lower Nyarong); Che Go Tsang of Shongshe; and Gyara Chipa of my clan. With my father were other sub-chieftains and dignitaries from the monasteries. They were all impressively dressed in their best clothes and attended by their retainers and servants. They were seated in order of rank on low ottomans covered with beautifully designed rugs. The courtyard was filled with the town folk, nomads, farmers, monks and people from all walks of life.

There was a hushed silence and the sound of many rustling brocade robes, as everyone rose to greet the victorious General Sonam Wangdue of the noble house of Khemey. He was a young man of stern countenance with sharp features, accentuated by a strong square chin. His long hair was tied up in a top-knot and secured with the turquoise brooch that signified his status as a Government official. By his side stood his second-in-command, Major Rugenma, who was a professional soldier and older than the general. He was a man of heroic proportions, whose appearance did every justice to the many stories of his incredible courage and boundless sagacity that were the common talk of Eastern Tibet. A hardened and experienced campaigner, it was said that he had climbed to his present rank virtually over the bodies of the Chinese soldiers he had killed in battle. All our chieftains filed past the two men and offered them ceremonial silk scarves as tokens of our respect. They also offered gifts of gold dust, pelts, brocades, entire carcasses of sheep and sacks of grain. Finally the chieftains resumed their seats. A prayer of thanksgiving was conducted by prominent lamas and a congregation of monks. Everyone participated in this expression of gratitude to the Dalai Lama and the gods of Tibet who had given us our freedom.

After the prayer, one of the oldest chieftains rose from his seat and recited the history of Nyarong, its geography and the lineage of its people, which according to our oldest traditions were handed down from father to son. He then made a warm but formal speech of welcome to the General and the Tibetan Army. The General in his turn made a brief, formal statement of thanks to the people of Nyarong for their loyalty to the Tibetan Government. He spoke softly in the Lhasa dialect, which was rather difficult for me to follow. But as he spoke slowly, and as we paid great heed to his words, I understood the importance of the statement he made.

"It is the wisdom and the labour of His Holiness the Dalai Lama that has reunited the people of Tibet under the lion banner of the ancient emperors. You are no longer under the alien rule of the Chinese tyrants, but instead you are now able to serve your own government, the Government of Tibet. Your good fortune today in returning to your land, where the most noble doctrine of the Lord Buddha holds sway, is due to the great efforts of His Holiness the Dalai Lama. It is therefore important that you should respect His laws, and pray for His long life and for the prosperity of the nation."

After this, they held a long ceremony in which all evil was symbolically driven away from our land and the gods thanked. Then a fire was lit and sprigs of sweet juniper were placed upon it. As the fragrant smoke rose to the heavens, everyone prayed. Then we flung handfuls of barley meal into the air, discharged rifles and in unison, shouted, "*Lha gyal lo!* Victory to the gods!"

At the end of the ceremony, one hundred men gathered in a circle and began to dance one of our old native dances, the *dro*. The men had thick turbans of yak hair around their heads, topped with red silk scarves. Their hair was decorated with coral, turquoise and archers' thumb-rings made of ivory. They danced sedately and majestically, with the long sleeves of their robes flying gracefully in the air as they sang the song of "The Auspicious Occasions."

> Above the gods and the thirteen auspices,
> The conch shell sounds from the distant temple.
> Oh, you yellow-hatted lamas and monks,
> If you sound the white conch like that
> You will surely invoke the luck of religion.
> Midst the gods and the thirteen auspices,
> Send the heavenly juniper smoke up in the sky.
> Oh, you men wearing fox-skin hats,
> If you burn such sweet incense
> You will invoke the luck of customs and law.

Below the gods and the thirteen auspices,
The women will serve us tea and ale.
Oh, you women with corals in your hair,
If you serve such excellent ale
You will surely invoke the luck of the feast.

And sure enough, there was much feasting and merry-
making after that. My mother and the rest of my family had
also come to celebrate, and it was a great holiday for us all. In
the evenings there was much singing and dancing, and good
chang flowed in abundance.

The young men and women, as usual, had a wonderful
time. We gathered in two groups, the girls on one side and the
boys on the other, and we sang love songs to each other.
When the boys finished a verse, the girls would try to outdo it
with a better one of their own.

Boys:
In the high sky, the road of the birds,
The best bird is the noble peacock.
Although you are a beautiful bird
I'll not ask you to descend,
But if you do, I'll certainly watch you.

In the town that is busy and big,
All the young people are my good friends.
Although they are beautiful
I'll not ask them to play,
But if they play with me, I'll certainly join.

Girls:
In the high sky, the road of the birds,
There are thousands of peacocks.
Will you watch every one of them,
Or will you desire only one.

In the town that is busy and big,
There are thousands of young people.
Will you play with each one you meet,
Or will you be true to only one.

And thus it carried on the whole night. When a particularly good response was sung, everyone roared with laughter and shouted their approval. The older men and women watched the youngsters having fun and sometimes joined them. Otherwise they sat around together gossiping, arranging marriages or praying softly.

Many of the chieftains were busy making arrangements with our new rulers; discussing supplies and transport for the army and also the policies of the new administration. I managed to strike up conversations with some of the soldiers. They were unanimous in their admiration of the courage of Major Rugenma, who on many occasions had spearheaded fierce attacks against the ranks of the Chinese army. The soldiers were also proud of their wily General, who, in the best traditions of Lhasan aristocracy, was so devious and shrewd that his stratagems had always confused and surprised the enemy. Some of them talked about Lhasa and its glories, the novelties and mysteries of that ancient city.

"That's where you ought to go, my boy" said a grizzled old sergeant. "A young lad like you would find much pleasure in the Holy City. There are the ladies, exquisite beyond belief, who would not ignore a strapping lad like you. Then there are 'the operas in summer and constant music in the taverns. As for the chang — there's no comparison. Of course I have nothing to say against the chang of this province; it is excellent, in a class of its own." He lifted his bowl and downed a good draft. Smacking his lips and warming to his subject, he expounded further on the virtues of the great city. "Of course, if you are in a religious frame of mind, there is the peerless cathedral, the great monastic universities and scores of other holy sites. It is enough to ensure that a man will never be rudely accosted by Uncle Shinje" (a popular term for Shinje Choegyal, or Yama Raj, the Lord of Death).

The festivities carried on well into the night and prodigious quantities of chang and *arak*, a potent and fiery whisky distilled from barley pulp, were consumed. My brother Wangchen was completely drunk. I drank only chang and kept away from the arak, despite the strenuous entreaties of the maidens who served the drinks. A tot or two is a welcome warm-up in winter, but it is definitely not a brew for steady drinking. My mother used to concoct a wonderful toddy on winter nights. She boiled butter with honey and served it piping hot into our bowls, which stood ready with small amounts of arak in them. This hot and invigorating brew was served to all, even the children. It made your insides all warm and comfortable and you slept wonderfully afterwards.

The following day, my father had a private audience with the General and he took me along. We went to the General's chambers inside the castle, where we were ushered in by one of his orderlies. The General welcomed us and bade us be seated. After receiving our ceremonial scarves, he and my father had a long conversation. My father told him that my grandfather had served the Tibetan government, and that he himself had been to Lhasa in the service of a government official. The General seemed most impressed and interested. He asked my father questions about the history and nature of the province and how the people had fared under Chinese rule. He also asked me questions about the terrain, wild-life and about my own experiences.

After three days we all returned home. It had been a great and momentous occasion, and I still could not get over my excitement. I seriously mulled over this new experience while on the back of my horse. What had struck me was the friendliness of the soldiers, so unlike the surly and miserable wretches that belonged to the Chinese army. I had also noticed how softly and politely the General spoke compared to most Chinese soldiers and officers, who had been extremely loud and boorish. Not only was the Tibetan General softly-spoken, but he had also spoken to us as equals. I mentioned this to my father and he seemed glad that I had noticed it.

"It is because we are of the same flesh and blood," my father said feelingly. "Although he is a noble man of a great and illustrious house, and an honoured official of the government, he is nevertheless a Tibetan like you and me — equal before the eyes of His Holiness the Dalai Lama. Therefore he spoke to us as brothers, and it is a thing no Chinese would have ever done. The Chinese consider us barbarians. I am glad that the first Tibetan government official you have met has been worthy of his great rank, because not all are so. Some of them are proud and rapacious. The Dalai Lama has punished and expelled many such people from His service, for their lack of consideration towards their own people. You must always bear in mind your great heritage, your race and your leader. Never forget your duty as a Tibetan and never give way to the enemy."

Over the small grove of shimmering trees, I glimpsed the roof of our house with its colourful prayer flags fluttering in the evening breeze. From far away came the distant bark of our mastiff, Rabshug, who had realised we were coming home. Our horses, sensing the proximity of their warm stables and full mangers, galloped over the steep path. We whooped and cheered, and the wind, catching our shouts, flung them throughout the purple hills.

3 Seasons

Spring has a first month, a second and a third
  month,
And a cuckoo sings out clear in the fields.
Summer has a first month, a second and a third
  month
And flowers bloom in the endless meadows.
Autumn has a first month, a second and a third
  month
And a swollen fruit drops silently from the tree.
Winter has a first month, a second and a third
  month
And the white ice grips the turquoise lakes.

Folk song from Ba, Eastern Tibet

If one could discount the bandits, the feuds and the Chinese, life on the whole was slow and rather pleasant for the common people. We had to work hard for a living, but we had enough time and wealth to celebrate our festivals, host occasional parties and picnics, and donate to the monasteries and temples. Of course there were the poor and the beggars, but they were not many and people were generous in our parts. Begging was not considered a dishonourable profession — after all, the Lord Buddha had begged. Many beggars in Tibet were sages in search of enlightenment, or pilgrims journeying to holy places. Otherwise, beggars were people who were too lazy to work, or too drunk most of the time to do anything else. There were very few people who were destitute due to misfortune or scarcity of work.

In accordance with the Tibetan calendar of the twelve beasts and five elements, the year began with *losar*, the New Year festival. This was the most important festival of the year, and a great deal of preparation went into making it an auspicious and happy event. In our home, we would clean all the rooms thoroughly and whitewash the walls. Large earthenware jars of choice ale would be prepared, as well as horns of prime arak and other good things to eat and drink. The New Year should fall on the first day of the first moon, as it does in other parts of Tibet, but in Nyarong, there is a complication that involves a little story.

Around the thirteenth century, there lived a saint called Sherab Gyalsten. He was greatly loved by the people and his fame spread far and wide. He was once invited by the Emperor of China to teach the words of the Lord Buddha at his court in Peking. The people of Nyarong were sad to see him go, but Sherab Gyaltsen promised to return to Nyarong before the New Year. Somehow, when it was time for him to come back, he was delayed. The people of Nyarong were so sad that they did not celebrate the New Year until he returned, on the thirteenth day of that month. So from then on, it became a custom for people to hold the New Year festival on the thirteenth day of the first moon. However, since it is necessary for the spring harvest to start ploughing the land by then, all the farmers conveniently celebrate the New Year on the thirteenth day of the twelfth moon of the previous year!

Anyway, the great day rolls in, and everybody gets up before sunrise and puts on their best clothes. Auspicious designs are drawn on the kitchen walls and incense is burnt in the hearth to honour the hearth spirit. At dawn, incense is burnt on the rooftops and religious banners are raised. These banners are decorated with the white feathers of a unique and beautiful bird called the *chakar*. Then there is an early morning feast of many courses. When the sun rises, the whole family goes on horse-back to the top of the hill above our village. There we burn incense to all the gods and spirits, particularly Dhunglo, the Conch Shell Spirit who ruled this particular hill. Our family are said to be descended from this spirit.

With all the formalities and the necessary rituals accomplished, there is continuous feasting and merry-making for three days. Then people from many villages gather to witness and partake in a competition of riding and shooting skills. Large tents and awnings worked with traditional designs are pitched on the side of a broad meadow. Each team of riders erects its own tents and there are separate tents for the women and children.

To warm up, the riders gallop past the field and pick up ceremonial scarves from the ground. Then the competition starts in earnest. Each rider is obliged to perform a series of acrobatics on his horse at full gallop. In the style called *ga chu*, the rider firmly grips the pommel of his saddle and jumps off to one side. The horse is galloping at full speed the whole time. In the *chaba*, the same sort of movement is repeated, but only one foot touches the ground. This is somewhat easier than the *gachu* but one is more likely to break one's feet. I broke mine when I was seventeen. Another style, *goser*, demands a great deal of nerve. With the horse thundering at full speed, the rider bends his body back to one side of the horse. He leans back until his face is very close to the pounding hooves, and his hands are nearly trailing on the ground. In this position he proceeds to pick up scarves from the ground.

In between the events, the riders swagger about at the side of the field, feigning indifference to the admiring glances of the women. Then from the back of their racing steeds, the riders shoot at targets with bows and rifles. They also shoot their rifles with one hand from under the running horse. At the end of the day, all the riders are presented with ceremonial scarves. My brother was a very good rider, and I was not too bad myself. When we were boys, we used to ride bareback on wild horses and yaks. Many a time we were ignominiously thrown on our backs and sometimes nearly killed. But we were never daunted. I guess it is as the proverb says: "A father cannot tell his son not to ride a wild horse, and the son cannot tell the horse not to throw him off."

There was also a lot of dancing and singing in the evenings. Games of chance like dominoes and dice were popular with the older people.

Around the first moon, all the fields are prepared for ploughing. Stones are removed and manure is hauled to the fields. Ploughing begins on the second moon, and a small feast is held on the land. Incense is burnt as an offering to the earth spirits and a special chang called Plough Chang is consumed. The fields are ploughed with a wooden plough which is tipped with an iron share. The ploughs are normally pulled by a powerful animal, the *dzo*, an extremely strong cross between a bull and a female yak. His strength is proverbial and he patiently and stolidly drags his plough forward, no matter how deeply the farmer pushes the ploughshare into the ground. Every family pampers its dzos, and they are fed more than substantially. During hard times the other animals and even the farmers may have to stint a little, but not the dzo; the prosperity of the family depends on his strength. Each family planted about eight to ten bags of seed grain, and the usual return was about twenty-five bags to each bag of seed.

Harvesting was not a haphazard enterprise with us. The whole village met and discussed the right time to bring in the crops. The older heads figured out the size and the firmness of the ears, and also the weather. Calendars and almanacs were consulted, and if possible the services of a sorcerer, preferably one of the Bon faith, the pre-Buddhist shamanist religion of ancient Tibet. As Bon sorcerers had long-standing and immutable ties to the old mountain and earth gods of Tibet, they had great power in controlling the weather.

Harvesting was a gay time because the whole village worked together, and friends and relatives from other villages came to help. Great pots of chang were brought to the fields, and there was much singing and feasting as the sheaves of golden barley were cut and stacked. Enormous meals were served to all, and when the work was done the young men and women

would tirelessly dance, sing and romance around a big bon-
fire.

Since there was no dearth of good things to eat and drink,
the gaiety would carry on late into the night. We were young
and strong then, and after only a few hours sleep we were
ready to face a new day of hard work.

Our usual crops were wheat, peas, soya beans, buckwheat,
potatoes, radishes, turnips and red peppers. Barley was our
most important crop. It was roasted and ground to make
tsampa, which is the staple diet of all Tibetans. Tsampa can be
prepared and eaten in a variety of ways. You can mix it with
tea and eat it in doughy balls, as is usually done, or you can
make it into a porridge and flavour it with meat and spices.
Even cakes are prepared with it, mixed with butter, cheese
and brown sugar. With some ingenuity, the possible recipes
for a tsampa-based meal are endless. It is great for taking
along on a trip as you don't have to cook it, and it never goes
bad or stale. Even if you couldn't afford anything else, you
could mix your tsampa with water, and it would make an
adequate meal.

Around the fourth moon is the festival of *Saga Dawa*,
which is the anniversary of the birth, enlightenment and death
of the Lord Buddha. On this day we would not eat meat, and
the whole family gathered together for long prayer meetings.

Around the fifth moon, the wild flowers are at their best,
carpeting the meadows with endless waves of bright blue and
yellow, and occasionally white and red. Then it was truly
summer. As the yaks grazed on these plants, the milk at this
time would carry a faint scent of wild flowers and the subtle
flavour of many herbs. It was also time for the festival of
Zamling Chisang, the Universal Offering of Incense. Our
entire family would camp out on the meadows up the hill,
and burn sprigs of sweet juniper as an offering to the gods.

At this time, we would take our animals high up into the
mountains to graze. We owned about sixty yaks and forty
sheep, which is a modest sized herd in Tibet. Nomads in the
highlands have much larger herds as they depend entirely on
their animals for their livelihood. I would go along with the

village lads, and with supplies to last us a few weeks we would camp out in the mountains with our animals. I remember how I sometimes used to quietly sneak out of the camp at the dead of night and silently ride away to meet some girl. Sometimes a little rain would fall, and my girl and I would huddle under my big felt cape, feeling very warm and happy. We would talk for hours and hold each other's hands.

On the tenth day of the sixth moon, a big celebration was held at the monastery of the Iron Knot in honour of Guru Rinpoche. The monks of the monastery performed elaborate and beautiful Tantric dances, symbolically depicting the life of the great saint Padma Sambhava and the trials he encountered when he first brought the teaching of the Lord Buddha to the Land of Snows. People from all over the province came to worship and attend these sacred performances, which lasted for many days.

For most young people it was a good opportunity to meet each other. There was a quaint custom whereby a girl would give her boot straps to the young man she most admired. These straps were pretty things, woven with coloured threads. Some young men would proudly sport nearly half a dozen of these romantic tokens. This often caused much envy amongst his friends, and sometimes grief and embarrassment to himself when he would be accosted by a number of indignant sweethearts. I guess young people all over the world behave as we did. We danced, sang, fell in love, grew jealous, showed off and did innumerable other silly and inconsequential things. We expressed feelings of the heart through songs, and our people seemed to have an endless store of these. Here are some that are quite obvious in their message:

> From the heart within my breast,
> I can think of only one thing,
> That is you, who have stolen my heart.

And when a girl appeals to her love to be true to her:

> The gossip in the village is like a tiger,
> The gossip in the family is like a leopard.

You, between the tiger and the leopard,
Your heart should always be firm.

A girl discovers her lover has other sweethearts besides herself:

The full moon of the fifteenth day rose in the east
And happily shone its first rays on me.
But on rising, its light spread wide
And now shines all over the world.

When a brash young man feels one sweetheart is not enough for him:

There is a long ornamented musket
  and a short rifle.
The long musket looks very attractive
  but the short rifle is more accurate.
I actually desire both of them.

And when the brash young man who wanted two girls is now left with none, and his first love is getting her own back:

Last year on the wide and grassy plain,
I saw you riding the blue horse in the morning,
I saw you riding the spotted white in the evening.
This year when I went to the wide and grassy
  plain,
You were without a single horse and going on foot.
Do you know this is your well-deserved fate?

Even now, I remember the smells of autumn — hay and dried leaves, the faint scents of the departing wild flowers and the fresh and resinous tang of the wood we chopped and stacked for the coming winter. I was not a very proficient axeman, and I always had blistered hands during that season.

This was also the time when we slaughtered animals for our winter meat supply. Sausages were stuffed, blood puddings jellied and some portion of the meat cut into small strips and dried. Most of the meat was hung in cold storerooms facing north.

In the tenth moon our family had a special prayer festival.

We invited about forty monks to our home to conduct certain prayers and rites for the well-being of the family.

After about a year, the Tibetan Army suffered drastic setbacks in its advance east. The retreating Chinese, now strengthened with reinforcements, pushed back our small army and finally poured into Eastern Tibet. It was a bitter day for all of us when our ancient Lion Standard was hauled down, and the red and yellow flags of the Chinese Nationalists flown from the Castle of the Female Dragon. Once again, my father was mad with rage and frustration and he stormed about the house cursing and swearing. For a few days we had to keep out of his way.

It was not the national defeat or the loss of our independence that affected me. I was too young, too ignorant and too expectant of the future to realize such things. It was more a bewildering personal sadness. Until the previous year, I had never seen our own army, I had never seen the ancient standard flying, I had never met, much less talked to, a real general. My young mind had identified totally with these things. It was my army, my flag, my general. Their conquests were my conquests, and I wanted to see them win even more — to march from one victory to another in endless glory. It was the dream of a young boy, and it disappeared like the soft morning mist when struck by the rays of the rising sun.

Our defeat was compounded the following year. On the night of the thirteenth day of the eleventh moon of 1933, the Water Bird Year, His Holiness Thubten Gyatso, the Thirteenth Dalai Lama, passed away to the Heavenly Fields. A great sadness fell upon the land. No sorrow could ever afflict us as did this one, and our setbacks of the previous year were forgotten. My mother took off all her ornaments and the whole family went into mourning. All the prayer flags were brought down and butter lamps lit in every house and on every roof. All the monasteries and temples in the province conducted special services, and we did the same in our house.

My mother, my aunt and the other women in the house all wept. It was a great effort for us men to hold back our tears ... some of the older ones could not.

The Thirteenth Dalai Lama had been a strong, wise and just ruler. He had gained Tibet's independence and was by degrees wresting the provinces of the east, including Nyarong, from the hands of the Chinese. He had created a modern Tibetan Army, which, though small, was well-trained and capable of fighting the much larger armies of China.

He abolished capital punishment and amputation which had prevailed in some regions. He curtailed the privileges of the aristocrats and the monasteries, and abolished many laws that were unfair to the common people. Inefficient, lazy and rapacious officials were removed from service and replaced by better men. Government officials were forbidden to gamble and drink heavily, and they were made to work hard and honestly for the state. Countless reforms were made in the monasteries and all the sects were required to remain pure and distinct. He improved and systematized all the old ceremonies and traditions, both religious and secular, thus giving the Tibetan people a focus for their aspirations and a renewed sense of belonging to their race and nation. We considered him the greatest and the best ruler that Tibet has ever had, and he was appropriately called the Great Thirteenth.

The entire nation took up a collection to build a mausoleum worthy of his greatness. Although our province was now under the Chinese, we collected a large amount of gold, silver and precious jewels which we sent to Lhasa as the contribution of the loyal people of Nyarong.

Gradually the people shook off their sorrow and went back to their daily lives. Yet there was a place in our hearts which was empty, and we prayed and hoped he would return to us soon.

When I was twenty, my parents wanted me to marry. They had already selected a girl, the daughter of the Chieftain Chigo Tsang, the clan leader of Khongshe. Although my family was a modest one and my father only the Arrow Chief of a sub-tribe, he had a great reputation as a scholar and a man of integrity. Thus the marriage was arranged and in the course of time, I was informed. I made a few protests just to show my parents that it was my marriage, and after an initial show of reluctance I finally gave my consent. The girl, Nyima Tso, was nineteen and very beautiful. At dances and festivals I had always tried to look my very best in her eyes. I think my parents must have known that. In a small community like ours, nothing could really be kept a secret for long.

The first thing that happens at this sort of wedding is the formal preliminary conference at which the two families meet and make the rather unromantic but necessary deals. This is accomplished in a traditional manner during a modest but formal banquet. Some years earlier both parties would have observed the custom of singing boasting songs. But because of the drinking common on such occasions, quarrels, fights and other inauspicious incidents used to occur and so this custom had been wisely discontinued.

My father had to pay the rather stiff price of thirty *dotses*, three thousand silver dollars for the girl. Since she was from a very prosperous family, her share of her family's wealth would be considerable, and so in the long run it would be no loss to us. In fact she brought in much more than we had ever expected. On a later occasion when my fortunes fell drastically, she generously gave up all her jewellery and ornaments to get me out of my predicament. But that is another story.

Fresh chang had been brewed, arak distilled and all other preparations made. Astrologer monks had been consulted, and since all the omens were favourable my wedding-day was finally arranged. The night before, Nyima and three other close friends had ridden to the girl's home to deliver a fine female yak, as a present for the girl's mother. This is known as the "milk price" and is supposed to compensate the mother for the loss of her daughter. They had also delivered the other required gifts of silk scarves, religious books and a brand new wooden basin for the girl to wash her hair in. A feast was then held, with much singing and dancing. When it ended they presented ceremonial scarves and packets of currency to all the young people present, as was the custom.

It was a fine morning, and I was waiting, dressed in a new outfit. Everybody in the house was rushing around putting final touches to the preparations, and the kitchen was a pandemonium of cooks, helpers and relatives. Everyone seemed to have something to do and no-one paid me any attention as I strolled around feeling somewhat nervous. Outside, lined up on either side of the pathway, were the old people of the village with casks of fresh water before them. This was considered auspicious, and they were to receive gifts from the bridal party. Most of the young people from the village had departed earlier to welcome the bride.

The bridal party appeared in the distance and my family and I went to receive them. The party halted at the boundary of our land, and one of my friends went over to lead the bride's horse over to our side and up to our house. She looked very beautiful in her silk robe and rich jewellery. Her dark shining hair was arranged in long plaits and decorated with coral ornaments. She wore a jewel-encrusted charm box around her neck.

She looked at me with her dark sloe eyes and smiled shyly. I smiled back and felt a great happiness in my heart. She dismounted onto a tea-chest covered with silk, and my mother led her into the courtyard, where both of them thrice circled a large barrel full of fresh water. Then we all sat down on mats and performed a short ritual prayer, conducted by the monks, to bring luck to the family. After this, the bride was taken to the kitchen where she was given a bowl of milk. She dipped the tip of her third finger into it, and flicked a few drops into the air as an offering to the gods. We were then both led to the family chapel where the monks and the lama, Chandi Rinpoche (my brother), gave us their blessing. Then we proceeded to the family Treasure House where the luck of my family was kept in the shape of a mystic arrow.

After all that, there was endless feasting for three hectic

days. My friends and relatives came to offer me and my bride their congratulations, ceremonial scarves and presents. Everyone, including my father, got truly and magnificently drunk and there was much singing and dancing. We have songs to suit every occasion, and marriages are no exception.

> The good steed is like a swift bird,
> The golden saddle is like its feathers,
> When the bird and its feathers are together
> Then the great Highlands are easily crossed.
>
> The ornamented musket is like thunder in the sky,
> The black powder is like lightning in the sky,
> When both lightning and thunder meet
> Then the high hills are illuminated.
>
> The young tiger man is like the sun,
> The young girl is like the full moon,
> When the sun and the moon meet
> There is happiness in the village.

After three days, we rode over to my wife's home where a similar ceremony took place. For three days they also held a great feast after which my wife and I returned home to begin our new lives together.

I have never found any occasion to doubt the wisdom of my parents' choice of a wife for me. Although happy marriages are more the exception than the rule, I guess I inherited my father's luck in this matter. Nyima Tso was a wonderful woman, more than I ever deserved. She was everything a man could ask for — beautiful, gentle, hard-working and religious like my mother. Though she had a streak of toughness in her, and did not readily agree with all my decisions, she was immensely loyal and stood by me till the last of her days.

4 To the City of the Gods

Although the Chinese had occupied Nyarong and other parts of Eastern Tibet, they had never been able to subjugate us or break our spirits. Despite political disunity and the constant feuding of the tribes, there were often sporadic outbreaks of rebellion against the hated invaders. On two occasions even the headquarters of the Chinese at the Castle of the Female Dragon was captured and the garrison thrown out. Remarkably, the person who performed these deeds was a woman.

The Gyari Tsang family was one of the oldest in Nyarong and they were the chieftains of the Upper Nyarong tribe. Chime Dolma was born into this family in the late eighteen hundreds and by her courage and sagacity soon became the leader. She was of medium height with a deceptively sweet face. She dressed like a man and always carried a pistol. During her life she conducted innumerable feuds and battles with other tribes. Her hatred of everything Chinese was enduring and intense.

In 1935, one detachment of the Red Army crossed Nyarong on their Long March to Shensi. Chime Dolma was then involved with internal feuds and hostilities against the Nationalist Chinese garrison in Nyarong. However, she decided to take on the Communists as well. She threatened dire consequences to all Tibetans giving or selling food to the Red soldiers. She would constantly harrass their detachments with sniping and sudden ambushes. She took her men and went south to Thau and engaged the Communists in a number of skirmishes. They managed to get the upper hand and she was forced to retreat north to Drango where she fought a great battle against the Communists at the local monastery.

Two other people were famous at this time for their valour against the Reds. One was Ako Heshey Gyatso, a nomad chieftain from Eastern Nyarong, and the other was Pon Nyuku Agen from lower Nyarong. Both of them had single-handedly slain prodigious numbers of Communist soldiers by sniping at their columns across impassable gorges and ravines. Ako Heshey Gyatso was reputed to have crossed the century mark with his kills, and Pon Nyaku Agen had shot about sixty Red soldiers. It is only fair to mention that during the Long March, many of the Communist soldiers were not well armed and were in a pretty sorry state anyway.

The Reds left after about four months and Chime Dolma turned her attention to more immediate problems. In 1936, she attacked the Castle of the Female Dragon and drove out the Nationalist garrison. She had to surrender the castle a few months later in the face of a bigger Chinese army. Chime Dolma was indomitable, for in 1939 she again attacked the castle and killed about fifty soldiers — the rest fled. She occupied the castle for four months, before the inevitable return of the Chinese.

This time, the Nationalist army was bigger than ever and they pushed her all the way back to her own tribal grounds in Upper Nyarong. They laid siege to her fort and finally burnt it to the ground. Chime Dolma was captured and taken in chains to the Castle of the Female Dragon, where she was incarcerated. She remained proud and defiant, even in her final moment before the firing squad. She was said to have cried out these words before she fell: "Never will I submit to the Chinese ... I die for the freedom of my people and my land. People of Nyarong, do not forget me."

In 1939, I fulfilled by boyhood resolve to visit the Holy City of Lhasa. For our people in Eastern Tibet it was the ultimate experience to see Lhasa at least once before we died. Lhasa was both the capital of our country and the centre of our culture and religion. Many monks from our province went there to study at the three great monastic universities of Sera, Ganden and Drepung. Indeed, some of the most renowned scholars, lamas and saints of Tibet have come from Eastern Tibet.

It is difficult enough to get to Lhasa on foot or horse-back as the way is filled with great dangers and hardships. Yet particularly pious folk, or people who have need of great penance like bandits or hunters, will accomplish this journey solely by prostrations. Pilgrims will stretch their entire body out on the ground, marking their furthest extent with a pebble. Then they rise, walk to the pebble and, picking it up, commence prostrations again. Their elbows and knees are padded with leather, and even these wear out on the long journey. It takes many years to fulfill this task, and they may die on the way — but the faith of our people is great.

Initially I went to Dhartsedo, the Tibetan town and trade mart on the frontiers of Tibet and China, to buy merchandise for selling in Lhasa. I bought silk belts and brocades, which I knew would appeal to the rich city folk. I also bought small cakes of Chinese ink, snuff and cheap knick-knacks like combs, needles and pocket mirrors. From Nyarong I took indigenous things that were in demand in Lhasa like the grass that yields a red dye used to colour sacrificial cakes, *tormas*, in temples and monasteries.

I was going to travel with the party of Pachen, the younger brother of the Gyara Chipa family and the chief of our tribe. My sister Dechen was to accompany me. We were nineteen people in all, and armed enough to deter any bandits. With the exception of two old men, all of us decided to walk in order to increase the merit of our pilgrimage. Our horses and mules would only be used to carry supplies and merchandise. Emulating the Lord Buddha, we decided as far as possible to beg for our food throughout the journey. We chose the northern route across the highlands, the home of the nomads.

One fine morning I said goodbye to my family and promised to light butter lamps for all of them in the sacred temples of Lhasa. My sister and I were given ceremonial scarves by my wife, my parents and all the other members of my family. Our tea cups were filled and left that way to ensure our safe and speedy return.

The whole journey took about fourteen months. We travelled slowly. There was no need to rush and we savoured and enjoyed each new experience the trip had to offer. We would rise before dawn, and in the chilly darkness have our breakfast of tsampa washed down with steaming hot bowls of butter tea. Then the mules and horses were saddled and loaded. Curses would stir the darkness when a surly mule refused to co-operate, and some exasperated soul would grimly mutter this old ditty:

> You mule wearing pretty ornaments on your
>   head,
> The day we go to the city of Lhasa in U*
> Do not make trouble on the way.
> For I have the saddle to press you down
> Even more, I have heavy loads to press you down.

Then we set off at a brisk pace to get the chill and stiffness out of our bodies. The birds were twittering in the red glow of dawn as slowly the sun rose and warmed our blood. Most of us fingered our beads and murmured soft invocations as we walked. *Om mani padme hum, om mani padme hum.* Hail the Jewel in the Lotus — the sacred mantra of Chenrezig, the embodiment of Mercy. *Om mani padme hum, om mani padme hum ...* we uttered a hundred, a thousand, a million times, to accumulate merit for ourselves and for all sentient beings in the universe.

As we plodded along we would talk to one another, often joking and laughing. Most Tibetans are easily provoked to laughter, and the slightest mishap or unusual incident would precipitate low chuckles or raucous guffaws: a mule taking a bite out of somebody's rear, the wind playfully blowing a hat

*U is the Tibetan province in which Lhasa is situated.

far out of reach, or even the sight of portly little marmots standing upright outside their burrows, staring seriously at us and chattering excitedly to each other ... Chirrk! Chirrk! ... Chirriiik!

I would often fall in with Pachen, who was a good friend of mine. He was around thirty, very brave and handsome. He was quite conscious of his qualities and walked with a pro-vocative and swaggering gait. He was full of fun and also a great singer. He enjoyed clowning around, though at times he was prone to irascibility. There was some bad blood between him and his elder brother Gyurme, and their wranglings had split the Gyara Chipa family and our tribe into two factions. Pachen had brought along his young son Gyashing Tsethar on the journey, and the little boy would run, skip and hop tirelessly beside us, occasionally asking strange questions and pitching rocks at anything that moved.

At around noon we would find ourselves a good camping site, preferably near a stream and good pasture land, and settle down for the day. We were usually rather tired by then and would wearily unload and unsaddle our animals, sending them off to graze. There is a saying in our parts, that a man who can be lively and spirited when unsaddling is a real man. Everyone had his chores, some went off to fetch water, others to collect dung for fuel and one man went to look for suitable stones for building a makeshift hearth. Since fuel was difficult to find, especially in the highlands, one mule always carried a load of fire-wood for emergencies. We also had a leather bag full of dry dung or kindling, in case it rained and the fuel was wet. We called this bag our companion, for reasons that will be obvious to any wet, hungry and exasperated traveller who has tried to build a fire with damp fuel on a rainy day.

With the aid of a goat-skin bellow we soon had a nice fire going, and as soon as the tea had boiled, one of us would wave a ladle in the air and shout "Hurrah!"

After a hot meal, we pitched our small travelling tents of water-proof cotton, and the older people would settle down for a snooze. The rest of us would stroll around and visit some small temple or hermitage in the vicinity. If there was any nomad encampment nearby, we would go to talk or to beg some butter and milk. Never was hospitality refused, and we would return their kindness with a few needles, combs and snuff which are scarce in these remote areas.

We always had our evening meal before sunset. As darkness approached, we sat smoking our pipes and chatting beside the dying embers of the fire. The stars would come out, one by one, until the whole sky was ablaze with their splendour. In our land the sky is so clear and the starlight so bright, that it even casts shadows. We would point out the constellations to each other: the Northern Belt (the Milky Way), *Minduk* (Pleiades), the Seven Brothers of the North (Ursa Major), and many others. These stars were also our clocks, and we would know when to rise by the position of the Seven Brothers. Then we laid our weary bodies down on our hard felt mats, using our loosened robes as blankets and the long sleeves folded as pillows. Sleep came easily to our tired bodies.

We arrived at the great Dzogchen monastery after a few days. From there we proceeded until we came to the Drichu, the Phantom River. We crossed this swirling body of water in a large wooden ferry that was carried downstream a few miles before it managed to get to the opposite bank.

For the last few days we had been in nomad territory and now we had come to the Highlands proper. It was an immense flat stretch of grassland, broken by low mountain ranges. The grass is sparse but tough and we believe it is much better for animals than the lush growth of the lowlands. This is the home of the *kyang*, the wild and graceful animal that resembles the ass. It is brownish-yellow in colour and travels in herds of hundreds. Unlike the plodding ass, the kyang moves in exquisitely nimble bounds. It is very shy, and at the least sign of humans, the herd will leap away, as if with one mind. There are also large herds of antelope that make good eating.

The giant Tibetan brown bear, the *dremu*, also lives in these highlands. He is much bigger than the ordinary black bear and his upper torso is thickly covered with hair, his long locks covering his red face. He is omnivorous but subsists mainly on the marmots that abound in these regions. The clumsy dremu is not a very skilful hunter, and his greed has given rise to a saying in Tibet: a person who through his own excessive greed incurs losses is said to behave like a "dremu catching marmots." The dremu, when hunting, tears up huge clods of earth over the marmots' burrows and when he catches one, instead of eating it he tucks it under his huge rump and looks out for others. When he reaches out for another marmot, the first one wriggles out from under him and escapes. Yet the dremu, blinded with greed, ignores the consequences of his avarice and continues to hunt marmots in this futile and inane manner.

The nomad of the north is a tough and self-reliant person. He is honest and well-bred, and if you can overcome his initial shyness and reticence, he will prove to be an extremely loyal and generous companion. When a nomad accepts someone as a friend, he hooks his right index finger over that of his friend and swears a sacred oath.

The nomads are not so different from the average Tibetan, but they do speak a different dialect. They seem almost immune to the cold, and even in winter many have their heavy sheep-skin robes knotted around the waist with torsos bare. The nomads cherish the freedom of the open spaces, and the young often prefer sleeping in the open air rather than in a warm, stuffy tent. They are not deterred by snow falls — in fact a blanket of snow serves as insulation. In the morning, the nomads will unconcernedly shake off the snow drifts and begin the daily chores, without even a shiver or the least sign of discomfort.

The nomads' tents are large and black, woven with heavy yak hair. Usually a low sod wall is constructed around it to keep out the winds. The space inside is partitioned by many boxes and has nearly all the comforts of home that we farmers have. The innermost room is usually reserved for the altar and for the old people. The main room is, of course, the kitchen. They build their hearths on top of two pairs of upright wild yak horns stuck in the earth like the four legs of a table. Although they have no firewood, they have dried yak and sheep dung, which is an excellent substitute.

A nomad exists solely from sheep and yaks. A fairly large nomad holding is referred to as *kar tri nak tong* or "ten thousand whites and a thousand blacks," meaning a collection of ten thousand sheep and a thousand yaks. A nomad is obliged to keep such a large herd to make up for the ravages of wolves, bandits and sudden snow storms that are likely to wipe out a large portion of the herd.

The yak is a truly wonderful animal, and an account of his benefits and uses in Tibetan society is lengthy and awe-inspiring. He is an excellent beast of burden and can also be ridden like a horse. Generally the aged and the infirm like to ride yaks as they provide a very smooth ride. He is tougher and more sure-footed than a mule and is much less complaining and recalcitrant. He can be yoked to the plough, though his hybrid offspring, mentioned earlier, is better. His thick fur and tenacity make him peerless for travelling through snow. His long hair can be shorn like wool and is made into various articles — ropes, tents, slings, coarse water-proof blankets, sacks, bags and the heavy black tents that are totally impervious to the most violent gales that buffet the highlands of Tibet. On his underside he has a growth of soft hair that falls off seasonally and is used to make warm clothing. His meat is more delicious and much more nutritious than beef or mutton. His skin is used for making saddle-bags and other leather goods, and since it is so tough it is also used to cover boxes and trunks, making them virtually unbreakable. Rawhide thongs of yak-skin are used to lash fences and other things, in place of scarce and expensive nails. Even his shaggy tail has its use as a fly whisk and duster.

The female dre gives an abundant flow of milk that is so high in butter content that it is generally yellow. It is an excellent drink when diluted, and has a faint aroma of herbs and wild flowers. Numerous dairy products are made with the milk, and the butter is packed in air-tight skin containers and used as a medium of trade, taxation and often given as gifts. The butter is used to illuminate homes and temples, for cooking, and when rubbed on the skin it insulates against the piercing blasts of freezing winds. Our elders tell an amusing story of how the most indispensable yak first came to Tibet.

He originally lived in the hot plains of India with his brother, the water buffalo. The clever yak one day told the water buffalo that he wanted to go north to fetch salt for them both. The yak asked the water buffalo for the loan of his hair, as his own would not adequately protect him from the cold winds of the north. The water buffalo, greedy for the promised salt, readily agreed, and the shaggy yak with his borrowed coat of hair proceeded north. The yak found the north to be a veritable bovine paradise, with its endless grasslands, fresh water and salt. He decided never to go back. That is why, until the present day, the poor water buffalo has no hair. And when you see him with his sad face and drooping head, you know he is still waiting for the return of his errant brother.

The nomad's diet consists mainly of dairy products; butter, various types of cheese, milk and yoghurt. He exchanges some of these for barley. Except for the droma, the nomad never seems to eat any vegetables or greens. Many of them look down on people who eat vegetables, calling them animals and grass eaters. But farmers and town folk are not without their little quips on nomadic eating habits. Since the nomad's diet is so heavy in protein and bereft of any kind of roughage, constipation is a very common problem. There are funny stories of the nomad's curses and entreaties to heaven, as he goes through the painful but necessary act of nature.

The nomad has a weakness for arak, when he can get it. The only time he can is when he comes down to the villages — and then he indulges. A nomad amazed and rather overcome by an excess of alcohol is supposed to have said, "This drink is truly wondrous: though I am without clothes, it makes me warm; though I am timid it makes me brave; and though I am stupid it makes me witty." Needless to say, this is a farmer's joke.

The nomad also keeps horses for herding his animals. He does not move very much and makes only seasonal changes in his pasture land. Most tribes are well-organised and the annual distribution of pasture land is a fair and democratic one in which all the families draw lots. Pasturage is divided into two kinds, the winter and the summer. Of course this organisation is not perfect and fights do break out occasionally. This occurs when a family feels that the lottery has been rigged or when a nomad gets furious with an unusually long run of bad draws. All the nomads are organised into tribes that are led by hereditary chieftains. Some tribes of Western Tibet and those north of Lhasa elect their chieftains. These elections are formally ratified by a representative of the Government, or the local governor. Many of the tribal chieftains are powerful and wealthy, possessing immense herds of yak and sheep. Some have tents capable of comfortably sheltering five thousand people. These massive and heavy tents are used for tribal gatherings and are transported in sections on the backs of yaks.

On our journey, we sometimes encountered a wild yak or two. The *drong* lives in the highlands, far from human habitation, and is a massive beast, his size greatly enhanced by his immense coat of thick black hair. He is generally around eight to nine feet at the shoulders; so big, in fact, that if you were lucky enough to kill one and gut him, you could step inside his massive frame and stand upright, only having to bend your head a bit. Since he is solitary and extremely truculent and fearless, he is difficult to hunt. This task is made even more formidable by the fact that he is nearly impervious to bullets. His dense shaggy coat is his first line of defence. Underneath that he has a thick, tough skin that grows hardest at the breast. His final armour is a subcutaneous layer of fat that stops any bullet that has managed to get through his hair and hide. Even his tongue is so rough it can rasp a person's skin. He is short-tempered, mean and born to fight, and since no other animal ever challenges him, he is obliged to battle with his own kind.

In the bleak and freezing wastes of the great highlands, a battle between two male drongs is a spectacle of epic proportions. Far away from each other, the two black behemoths shake their massive horns and paw at the hard ground furiously, in their pent up rage. As if at a signal, they lower their heads and charge. The earth trembles under their pounding hooves, and the little marmots in their burrows chatter in fear. Building up momentum, the two great beasts now rapidly close in on each other. Their heads meet with the crash of thunder and their locking horns resound like falling rocks. Boulders would be pulverized in such a collision, but the two giants are not bothered and back off for another charge. Finally, after a number of charges and collisions, one of the drongs is dazed, and retreats. The proud victor tosses his adamantine head, as if challenging the very heavens.

Despite the obvious dangers, he is hunted by humans. His body can provide more meat than three or four yaks, and a yak is no small animal. It is a sign of great bravery and prowess for a hunter to bring down one of these animals. Such a deed is worthy of a song:

> When I went to the bright rocky hills
> A yellow-mouthed drong charged at me,
> A wild yak with swinging horns — and very
>   angry.
> But I greeted him with my ornamented rifle
> And killed the drong, his horns struck the earth.
> Do you know this, O listener?

It must be a close shot and you must hit him from the side, through the lungs. A head shot is no use. The bullet will just ricochet off that diamond-hard skull, and the heart is too well protected. Unskilled hunters with little courage attack the drong in large bands, and pour a hail of lead on him until he drops. This crude method has no guarantee, and there have been incidents when after receiving forty or more bullets this gallant beast has attacked his assailants and killed or maimed them.

The great horns of the drong are much prized. They are chased with silver, ornamented with coral and turquoise, and used as receptacles for arak and ale. The nomad uses the hard skin of the breast as a chopping board. In the highlands there are no trees at all, so the nomad of the interior makes his tent poles with the skin of the drong. He takes the raw hide and cuts it into long strips that he sews together with gut into long tubes. He then stuffs the tubes tightly with wet sand and sews up the ends. The tubes are left overnight to freeze. The water in the sand expands to ice and the tubes are drawn tight. Finally they are dried in the sun until the skin hardens and becomes like steel. One end is cut open and the loose sand shaken out. The result is a light tube which is as strong as metal, and capable of supporting the nomad's heavy tent.

About three days from the Phantom River, we reached the trading centre of Kyikudo. It is a relatively large town from where the major portion of the Tibetan tea trade is conducted. All caravans going east to China pass through this town, as well as most caravans from Lhasa to Eastern Tibet. Thus it is one of the biggest caravanserais in the whole of Tibet. Although it was a Tibetan town, Kyikudo had been conquered by General Ma Pu Fang, the Chinese Muslim (Hue Hue) warlord who had also conquered and occupied the Tibetan province of Amdo. Just outside the town was the famous shrine, inexplicably called the Mani of China. The "Mani" is the mantra of Chenrezig, *om mani padme hum*. It was an open spot filled with stones of every conceivable size, every one of them bearing the sacred inscription *om mani padme hum*. A community of stone carvers who lived nearby did all the sacred inscriptions. Pious people would buy an inscribed stone from them and place it on the ever growing

collection, to acquire merit. From Kyikudo, we continued
our journey on the Tea Road to Lhasa.

We trudged on slowly and pleasantly, exploring new
places, and visiting strange and remote hermitages and temples. Around the eighth moon, we arrived at the important
nomad centre of Nagchukha. This little town is also the
Government headquarters for the whole of Northern Tibet
(Hor) and is a busy junction for travellers and merchants.
What made it important for us was that from here it was only
ten days walk to Lhasa.

At Nagchukha we made a wonderful discovery. The fourteenth reincarnation of His Holiness the Dalai Lama had been
discovered in a village in Amdo, and he had been conducted
back to the City of Gods with great rejoicing and ceremony.
Just a month before our arrival, His Holiness and his entourage had crossed Nagchukha to Lhasa. The lucky people of
Nagchukha and the surrounding areas had built tall earthern
incense burners all along the way, and the road to Lhasa had
been marked with white stones and auspicious designs drawn
in powdered chalk. We thanked the fate that had brought us
on a journey to Lhasa at this time, and with happy hearts and
light feet we set off again. We crossed the Nyenchen Thanglha or the Trans-Himalayan range, and descended into the
valley of the Kyichu or Happy Waters. It was in the ninth
moon that we first saw the golden spires and canopies of the
Potala, the Winter Palace of the Dalai Lamas, from far in the
distance, and our hearts stopped in awe, reverence and fulfil-
ment.

We prostrated on the ground three times and thanked the
gods for bringing us safely to the Holy City. I do not think
there is a structure like the Potala anywhere in the world. To
me it seemed as if the massive palace had grown out of the hill
like a living thing, and that it was a natural part of the hill and
the summit of our land.

We entered Lhasa from the eastern suburbs of Ba Nak
Shod after crossing the small Mindol bridge. In accordance
with a custom observed by the people of Eastern Tibet, we

did not pause to find lodgings or even drink a cup of hot tea, but made straight for the Great Cathedral. There, we paid homage to the Jowo, a statue of Buddha Sakyamuni, the most sacred image in the whole of Tibet and the source of countless miracles. We offered many butter lamps and prayed long and earnestly.

Lhasa appeared strange and wonderful to me. I had never been to a city of its size and diversity, and I relished every novelty it had to offer. The narrow streets were crowded with people from every part of Tibet. There were tall Amdowas, swarthy men from Kongpo in the South, squat Bhutanese and groups of wide-eyed nomads looking very lost and forlorn. Occasional Mongols and Chinese passed through the streets, while humble pilgrims, monks and nuns, peasants, beggars and aristocrats in gorgeous silken robes rubbed shoulders as they went about their business. There were shops everywhere, overflowing with goods of every kind, and the voluble and articulate shop-keepers shouted their bargains across the streets. We visited all the sacred places, made offerings and lit butter lamps. Guided by a monk friend of ours, we made a tour of the Potala Palace. The interior was more like a town than a building, and there were countless sacred images and relics. We also paid homage to the mausoleums of the Dalai Lamas which were covered with beaten gold and encrusted with precious jewels. The endless corridors and innumerable rooms and halls of the Potala would have baffled and confused anybody. Without our guide we would surely have got lost in that gigantic maze.

We also visited the School of Medicine on the Iron Hill, Chakpori, just next to the Potala. There we paid our respects to the many sacred objects, the most wonderful being the images of Chenrezig, the Goddess Tara and the deity Amitayus, fashioned respectively out of conch, turquoise and coral. We moved around Lhasa for a number of days, visiting various other holy and historical sites.

After some time, we decided to move on. We left our horses and mules and most of our baggage at our lodgings (the home of a merchant friend from Eastern Tibet). Carrying our necessities on light willow pack-frames, we set out to visit the other holy places in Central Tibet. Our first stop was Samye, where the first Buddhist temple in Tibet was built, and then to the nearby monastery of Mendoling. We then journeyed south to the Yarlung valley, the cradle of Tibetan civilization. From there we proceeded to Densatil, the great monastery of the Phagmodrupas, a dynasty of Lamas that ruled Tibet in the thirteenth century. We also visited the monastery of Sang Ri Khamar, built by the great female saint Machig Labdron. At Lhobdrak, the home of the venerated Marpa the Translator, we paid our respects to the memory of this great guru and his most famous disciple, Milarepa. Milarepa was made to build many houses single-handedly, and to tear them down again, in order to expiate his sins. His task master and guru, Marpa, allowed only one of these structures to remain standing. An old nine storey house, now a temple, still stood as a symbol of the great tenacity, strength and faith of Milarepa. After a day's journey from Lhobdrak, we reached the monastery of Lhalung Pedor, the monk who assassinated the apostate king of Tibet, Lang Darma. At the town of Gyangtse, we circumambulated the great stupa of Pengoe Choeten. Proceeding to Sakya, we visited the monastery there, and paid homage to the memory of Sakya Kunga Gyaltsen, who reunited and ruled Tibet after the disintegration of the Tibetan Empire. Finally we reached the great monastery of Tashi Lhunpo, the residence of the Panchen Lamas, and paid reverence to the many holy relics and objects there.

We returned to Lhasa just before the New Year celebrations. Immediately after the New Year, the Great Prayer Festival took place. This festival, instituted by Gyalwa Tsongkhapa, the founder of the Gelugpa order, is a bid to hasten the coming of the Buddha of Boundless Love, Maitreya. All the monks of the great monastic universities come to Lhasa during this period, and the authority of the city magistrate is transferred to the monk proctors of Drepung Monastery for the duration of the festival. It is a very colourful and majestic festival, with many wonderful processions, elaborate and spectacular rites and ceremonies. This year, the festivities were on an even grander scale as the coronation of the Dalai Lama was to take place simultaneously. It was a happy occasion for the whole of Tibet and the people celebrated it with great joy.

The coronation, the Ascent to the Golden Throne, took place inside the Jewel Park, the summer palace of the Dalai Lamas, and the public were not permitted to enter. Afterwards there was a grand procession from the Jewel Park to the Potala. It was a rich, colourful and awe-inspiring spectacle. The government officials of various ranks in their splendid robes and headdresses, were followed by people in costumes that dated back to the early days of the Tibetan Empire. Some of them wore long coral ornaments with stones the size of fists. There were horsemen in ancient armour resplendent with swords, lances and shields, and columns of red monks carrying banners, parasols and many other ritual objects made of rare and costly materials. Words cannot describe it all — the colours, sounds, the excitement and most of all the great pride and reverence that filled the hearts of every one of us there.

All the people who had made contributions towards the Prayer Festival were permitted an audience with the Dalai Lama. Pachen had made such a contribution, and as I and some others had chipped in, we all made preparations to pay our respects to our great ruler. In a magnificent hall in the Potala, he looked down at us sternly as we prostrated before him, and he blessed us with a tassel-tipped stick. He was five years old at the time.

The number of sacred spots in Lhasa is endless, and I will not describe all the places we visited. Apart from our devotional tours, we sold all our merchandise, and in turn did a large amount of shopping. I bought a lot of woollen cloth, carpets, Indian cotton, corals and gifts for members of my family and friends at home. For myself I purchased a fine German Mannlicher rifle.

At the end of the fifth moon, we paid our final respects and homage to the Jowo in the Great Cathedral, and set off for home. We reached Derge around the eighth moon and we dispatched an advance rider to inform our families and friends that we were finally coming home.

5 Man of the Family

Great sadness was awaiting me when I returned home. Both my parents had died while I was away. Although their funerals had been taken care of by my brother and my wife, I did not feel it was enough to honour their memory. I had special services and prayers said for them, offered thousands of butter lamps, made substantial donations to the nearby monasteries and distributed alms to the poor and needy. All this was a considerable drain on our family wealth, which to begin with was not very great. However, this is what I wanted.

A few months later, another problem arose within the family. My brother Wangchen wanted to leave and begin a life of his own with a woman from a distant neighbourhood. I pleaded with him to stay, but he was adamant. Finally I relented and we got down to the unpleasant business of dividing our patrimony. My brother wanted just enough to start a decent life and had no desire to split the family wealth or to see our fortunes decline. I decided to give him all the yaks and sheep and asked him to leave the land and the rest of the property intact with me. Even then, I knew it would be rough going. Yaks and sheep are necessary for a farmer, as their dung is the only source of manure for the fields. Besides, I had my wife and the rest of the family to support. But my brother replied that he had no desire to become a nomad and agreed to take the equivalent amount in cash. I managed to pay him the sum by borrowing heavily from the monasteries and from some of my acquaintances. And so my brother went off to seek his fortune and I became the master of the household.

When my wife and I examined our accounts, we discovered our state of affairs to be in a deplorable condition. I had spent more than I had anticipated on my journey to Lhasa. The many offerings in the holy places and the numerous presents purchased had obliged me to borrow money from traders in Lhasa. My parents' death and subsequent funeral arrangements besides other matters, had also greatly increased our debts. But the biggest blow of all came from my brother's departure. We were now badly in debt. The only reassuring thing was that the family land and animals were still intact. I knew however that I would also lose this if I could not pay back my debts. All my creditors were extremely sympathetic and never tried to pressure me. Still, I realised I could not take advantage of their generosity indefinitely, and I resolved to find a way of repaying them as soon as possible. There is a proverb that says, "When the father dies, the son becomes a man." I now had to shoulder all these responsibilities and the burden of the household alone.

It was my wife who worked out a plan of action. She decided that as we could not repay our debts from our normal sources of income (our harvests, etc.), I would have to trade. I protested, as we did not have any capital. But my wife pointed out that she still had her jewels and ornaments. I was not keen on this idea, but finally she persuaded me. And so, leaving her and the other family members to look after the land and the herds, I set off with my wife's jewels to begin my short career as a trader.

There was a bustling trade between China and Eastern Tibet, most of it conducted at the Tibetan town of Dhartsedo near the Chinese frontier. One of the Tibetan exports was deer horns of various kinds, the best being the soft new growth after the deer had shed its old horns. These horns were prized by the Chinese for their geriatric remedies. The pods of the musk deer and bear gall were also in great demand as medicine, as well as the sex organs of deer which were used as aphrodisiacs. Deer were prized for the sinews of their feet for medical purposes, and even the unborn foetus was highly valued as a palliative during pregnancy. Medicinal plants were also in great demand in China, the foremost being the white root *bhimu*, and the bizarre plant called *yartsa gunbu*, which in summer is a stalk of grass and in winter metamorphosis into an insect. Eastern Tibet exported a variety of herbs, leather, woollen goods, pelts, salt and gold.

From China we bought tea, silks, brocades, snuff, smoking tobacco, textiles, guns and ammunition, and a host of other minor items like needles, combs, mirrors, china cups, etc. I followed the normal trader's pattern and went to Dhartsedo to make my purchases. Bad luck, inexperience and also the dominance of big traders badly affected my business. I also made the mistake of emulating the business practices of the rich merchants with my rather humble capital. After a year, I showed no profits. In fact, I had incurred some minor losses.

But my luck changed, or as we say, "my wind horse started running." On a tip from a friendly trader I went south to Lithang, which is only a few days journey from the borders of Yunnan. A great deal of opium was available at this place, imported from the poppy fields of Burma and Yunnan. I bought large consignments relatively cheaply there and transported them to the goldfields of Upper Nyarong, Thau and Drango. My customers were mostly Nationalist army officers, who retailed it to their soldiers and the Chinese coolies working at the goldfields. They also exported large amounts of it to China. The profits were incredibly large, although it was a difficult and dangerous sort of business. The distances involved were long and the terrain treacherous. Many bandits infested the waysides, and generous portions of graft had to be circulated among the Chinese officials involved. Somehow I managed to stay alive and also to make a considerable profit. After a year, I repaid all my debts and put aside a tidy sum for my family.

My wealth was not enough "to build a bridge of silver," but my family wanted to celebrate my good fortune, and so we decided to go on another pilgrimage to Lhasa. It was mainly my wife's desire to visit the Holy City, as she and the other members of my family (with the exception of my sister) had never been there. So with my wife, my youngest brother Chandi Rinpoche, Nyima and most of the servants (about twenty people in all), we left for Lhasa. On this journey we travelled in grander fashion, and all of us were on horseback. We took the middle route this time, crossing Chamdo. The whole journey took us about a year. We left Dhunkhug in the autumn of 1944, and upon completing our pilgrimage returned through the great monastery of Sok Tsenden Gon, The Sandlewood Monastery, around the tenth moon of the following year.

In 1946 I built a new house and all my friends and relatives were happy to see my family prosperous once again. There was only one sadness in my life — my wife could not conceive a child. She was always saddened by this fact, and made many offerings to the monasteries and temples, praying constantly for a son. Her main reason for going to Lhasa was to pray for a son before the most sacred Jowo Sakyamuni Buddha in the Great Cathedral. But no child was granted to us.

In our land it was considered a great misfortune not to have a child, especially a son, to carry on the family line. A man's wealth was first and foremost measured by the number of sons he had. It was a matter of survival. Strong hardy sons were needed in every family, to work and to fight bandits and settle feuds. Thus all my relatives and friends commiserated with me and many of them advised me to take a second wife. Although it was not contrary to our custom, I was reluctant. I dearly loved my wife and knew that a second woman in the household could mean unhappiness for all of us. My wife, in her sensible and matter of fact way solved the problem, and one night she confronted me with her solution. "I do not like to see you sad because of my barrenness," she said. "Marry again and we may yet have a son in this family."

"No," I replied, "I have thought this matter over many times, and I have no desire to take another wife. Do not be upset. It is our karma."

"I too have thought over this matter," she insisted, "and I

know what troubles you. You feel that if another woman came to our house there would be unhappiness between me and her. But it is not necessary that it should be so. If the woman were one that both you and I liked, and if she were close to me, I see no reason for any problems. You know I have a younger sister and she is now seventeen, old enough to be betrothed. I am very fond of her and it would make me happy if you were to accept her as your wife."

I knew that this was the best solution to the problem. I also knew that my wife's sister was a healthy young girl, she was well bred and we would have very little trouble with her. "I will think this matter over," I said.

My wife got up to go to the kitchen. At the door, she paused and added. "My mother knows about this. She and my sister both desire it should be so. You have been very good to me, better than most men are towards their wives. My mother likes you and she feels you would always do what was best for her daughters ... Please do it. Marry my sister." She then left to prepare dinner.

I was glad to know that my wife and her family were happy with the way I treated her. Although I agreed with my wife's sensible plan, I wanted to think things over and did not make my decision immediately. That procrastination proved to be the source of a great problem.

I went and talked this matter over with my tribal chieftain and friend, Pachen of the Gyara Chipa family. He appeared greatly pleased with my wife's suggestion and encouraged me to marry her sister. As I was leaving, he said he could see no problems whatsoever, but that I should nevertheless think things over carefully. He was normally a most impetuous sort of character and I felt glad he was thinking soberly for my sake.

After a few weeks, I went to see Tenzin Drakpa, my wife's elder brother and the head of the Chigo Tsang tribe. He was a very close friend of mine, but he seemed embarrassed and puzzled when I approached him about this matter.

"But she is already spoken for," he said, perplexed. "Why,

just two weeks ago Gyara Chipa Pachen approached me and asked for her as a bride for his son. I am very sorry about this, but I have given my word. The matter has been arranged."

I then realised that I had been very naive with Pachen, and that he had well and truly taken advantage of my confidence. My anger felt like "gall in the mouth and hair in the eye," and I resolved not to let him have his own way. I sent my wife to her home, supposedly for a holiday, but actually as a part of my plan. I learned that her mother was not too happy with the latest developments. The Gyara Chipa family, although our tribal chieftains, were at that time split amongst themselves and were an unhappy family. So when my wife revealed my plan to her, the old lady wholeheartedly subscribed to it. The object of all this controversy, my young sister-in-law Sonam Dolma, was also taken into confidence. She was gladly willing to be my bride. My wife had always spoken highly of me to her family, and that had most probably decided the girl on her future. According to plan, my old mother-in-law and my wife declared that they wanted to go on a short pilgrimage. Taking my future bride with them, they set off for our pre-arranged meeting place. I sent some of my men and they brought my bride to our home.

I knew that there was going to be trouble and had prepared for that eventuality by sending all our expensive and precious articles to a distant monastery for safe-keeping. Although I had theoretically abducted their daughter, I knew my wife's family would remain neutral in the coming feud. Gyara Chipa could out-gun and out-man me in every way, and it was obvious that things would be very sticky for me. The rift in the Gyara Chipa family was some consolation as Pachen would not be all that strong. Yet he could muster together more than two to three hundred men and rifles, while my friends, servants and myself could barely total sixty men.

Inter-tribal relationships are extremely intricate and involved with jealousies, hatreds and fears. Playing on these aspects, I managed to get more allies and also to borrow a few rifles and some ammunition. Finally, my position, though bad, was not hopeless.

The chieftains of the four major tribes of Nyarong were called *tongpons* or "leader of a thousand." This institution had been set up in the ancient days by the Tibetan Government for purposes of administration and taxation. Each tongpon was theoretically the ruler of a thousand families, but discrepancies had crept in through the ages, and the numbers varied from tribe to tribe. The tribes were divided into *denshoks* or sub-tribes, ruled by a *dhapon* or "arrow chief." The size of these denshoks varied from sixty to three hundred families. The tribal chieftain also had a personal denshok called the *nangde*. The denshoks were traditionally autonomous and actual power generally rested in these compact units rather than in the larger, more loosely knitted tribes. Sometimes, an energetic and ambitious tribal chieftain would try to increase his power and actually take over weaker denshoks. The Gyara Chipa family had in this manner subjugated two denshoks and had actual power over about five hundred families.

The first move was Pachen's, and although he did not act immediately, I knew he was preparing. People were shaking their heads at my folly, and predicting that I would come to a bad end. Some of them quoted an old proverb:

> Leaping where the tiger springs,
> The grey fox will break his back.

Guns were kept constantly loaded at my home and guards were posted to keep watch. I also had trenches dug around the house and barricades set up on the tracks. I had to be very careful as Gyara Chipa's land and mine were very close to each other's, divided only by the Nyachu river. For a few weeks there was a stalemate. Then one night I set off north to Kanze with my whole family and eight men. My old friend and present enemy, Pachen, was then in a double bind. Custom dictated that he avenge himself upon me. Yet I had contracted so many alliances with other tribal chieftains who were not friendly with him. Pachen knew that if he started something the consequences would be very bloody for all concerned. This would normally not have deterred a hot-headed man like him, but he knew his family was weak because of his quarrel with his brother Gyurme; and also as I was in Kanze with the powerful Shiba Tsang family, he would have to carry the war up north, thus entailing new problems.

After a year, some of the chieftains and a prominent citizen, Gyari Palden Gyatso managed to arrange a meeting between me and Pachen. Since my younger wife had already been promised to the Gyara Chipa family (they had even paid a dowry for her), I had to compensate them. We finally agreed on an indemnity of twenty thousand silver dollars. I presented Gyara Chipa with eleven horses, four rifles and other goods totalling the agreed sum.

After the truce I met my brother-in-law Tenzin Drakpa who playfully scolded me: "Aten, you old troublemaker, you gave us a very trying time." His eyes twinkled. "Old Pachen dug for a marmot and unearthed a fierce badger. Anyway, things have ended well, and I am glad you came out best. I couldn't help you before, as you had in a sense wronged my family. But if Gyara Chipa tries any tricks after this truce, you can count on me for help. You have two of my sisters now, and I guess that makes us one family."

I still remember Tenzin Drakpa's kind words, and I guess it is karma that united me with his young son Kesang Sherab or Agen here in India. Kesang has no family any more and neither have I. It is thus fitting that he and I should live together as father and son. He has since married and has children to carry on the blood of our two families.

Peace was thus restored. I was not too sure of Gyara Chipa's integrity and the value of the peace that I had purchased with silver. So I decided to remain in Kanze for some time until I could be sure.

Kanze was quite a large town, and was at that time under Chinese administration. During World War II the Nationalists had built a rough but motorable road up to this place and had also begun work on an airfield. The Tibetan inhabitants of this town had seen many armies of various Chinese regimes tramping through their streets. I was there on that early spring day in 1950 when the first Communist divisions marched through Kanze into Tibet.

6 Communist Invasion

Walking on a high and lonely ridge,
I met a strange new spirit,
I raised new banners for him
I offered sweet incense to him
But alas, he was a malicious demon,
And I am here, helpless.

Folk song from Nyarong

When the Communist army invaded Eastern Tibet, most of it
was already under the rather desultory occupation of the
Nationalist Chinese. By the end of 1949, Chiang Kai Shek
and the remnants of his Nationalist forces had been driven
from the mainland to seek refuge on Formosa. Thus the
various Nationalist garrisons in Eastern Tibet were left dis-
organised, demoralised and scattered, each having to decide
what to do in the face of an advancing and victorious Red
Army. In some garrisons, all the officers and soldiers openly
went over to the Communist side. Some put up a token
resistance and then quietly surrendered. Only a few tried to
hold out — and even in these garrisons, the tired soldiers
mutinied, shot their brave but foolhardy officers and deserted
en masse. Most of them did the most obvious and sensible
thing; they dropped their weapons, tore off their uniforms
and went home. I heard that a group of soldiers and officers
fought their way from Dhartsedo through Lithang and managed to escape to Burma.

To us Tibetans it made no difference. Chinese armies under
many regimes had come and gone through our land. All of

them had been brutal and tyrannical, yet thankfully indifferent, inefficient and corrupt. Of course we expected some changes in the beginning, but then we anticipated that the Reds would settle down, reveal their all too human weaknesses and leave us Tibetans alone.

The first Red soldiers entered Kanze on the night of the second moon in 1950. As the road built by the Nationalists was rough and incomplete, the soldiers came on foot, in straggling and endless columns. I was not too impressed. Most of them were dressed in shabby rags and armed with a motley collection of fire-arms, which despite their diverse origins were relatively modern. Yet what the Communist Army lacked in quality, they seemed to make up for in size. For a week, the long columns never ended.

I soon discovered the errors of my initial assessment. The Red soldiers were extremely well disciplined. They were the first Chinese soldiers I had ever seen who did not loot and bully the populace. Instead, the soldiers were courteous to the extreme, and even went out of their way to help the local people with their harvests and other chores. It was a pleasant novelty.

The commander of the Nationalist garrison and chief administrator of Kanze and occupied Eastern Tibet had been a most unpleasant, greedy and foxy old soldier. When he first learned of the debacle of the Nationalist Army and the advance of the Reds to Kanze, he suddenly declared himself to be a true and ardent Communist and flew a makeshift Communist flag from the top of the old fort. Some of his officers, loyal to the Nationalist Government, openly quarrelled with him. Somehow he managed to smooth things out and he formally arranged a lavish welcome for the first Red detachment which entered Kanze. He valiantly tried to convince the rather sceptical Communist officers of his newly acquired enthusiasm for the Marxist cause. Whether they believed him or not, that was the last we ever saw or heard of him.

When I returned to Dhunkhug, I learned that the Communists were already installed in the Castle of the Female

Dragon. I met the new military governor of Nyarong on the seventh moon of that same year. All the chieftains, Arrow Princes and other leading dignitaries of Nyarong were summoned to the castle. Our new ruler was a stout, taciturn man called Kao Thu Pen or Kao — the Military Governor. On this first meeting he did not talk too much about Marxist theories. Instead, he told us what we knew too well; that the Nationalist Bandit Regime was rotten, parasitical and finished for ever. He repeatedly stressed that the only thing the Communist government wanted was to better the conditions of the ordinary people and to remove the vices of the past. He made it clear that the present order favoured the rule of the people themselves, and that we, the local leaders, were to play the most important role in the regeneration of our society. We dutifully nodded our heads and murmured our assents.

On October 7th 1950, the People's "Liberation" Army crossed the Phantom River and marched into the part of Tibet that was under the administration of the Tibetan Government. The small Tibetan Army was defeated at Chamdo and the Tibetan Government in Lhasa surrendered. The Red Army marched into Lhasa, the most holy of cities, at the end of October.

A year after their arrival, the Communists set up a "People's Government." The whole of Nyarong was relegated to the position of a district, or *hsien* as the Chinese termed it, and divided into four sub-districts called *chue*. The chue were more or less the same as previous divisions of the four great tribes. The district headquarters were at the Castle of the Female Dragon. The Chinese also appointed Tibetan administrators for each chue. These were the old chieftains and the other notables of the country. In our sub-district of Wulu chue, Gyurme of the Gyara Chipa family and the elder brother of Pachen, was appointed administrator. I was given the post of assistant administrator. Nima of the Gyara Tsang tribe, was made the chief administrator for the whole of Nyarong. The Chinese paid generous salaries to all "officials," and I received the stipend of a hundred and twenty silver dollars a month.

Thus, except for terminology, the Chinese (at least for the time being) left the old hierarchy pretty much the same. Towards the end of 1951, I was sent with some Chinese officers to all the villages of Wulu chue on a publicity mission. We were to propagate the Chinese goal of converting Tibet into a "democratic" nation. The Chinese, at this time, constantly stressed the policy of "self-determination and self-rule." They emphatically stated that the Chinese had only come to teach the Tibetans how to rule themselves. When this objective had been achieved, they would return to their own country. Another more prosaic reason for our mission was to recruit labourers. The Chinese were building a new airfield at Kanze and they needed to transport large amounts of supplies (mainly ammunition) to Derge Yhilung, for the divisions that were invading Chamdo.

In nearly all the villages, the people listened to the political talks passively. But when they were informed that they would have to assist the Chinese in building the airfield at Kanze and also haul supplies, murmurs of anger and frustration filled the meetings.

"It takes four days to reach Kanze and more than ten to Derge Yhilung," they complained angrily. "We have our fields and herds to take care of, and anyway we have no desire to perform such labour. We have never done this kind of work. We refuse to obey such orders."

Undeterred by this protest, the Chinese simply threatened the poor villagers with armed reprisals if they did not comply. In the face of such persuasion, the villagers were in no position to refuse. The Chinese, however, scrupulously compensated the villagers for their labour with adequate wages.

In 1953, Kao the Military Governor left and we were put under civil administration. Our first party representative was called Wu the Commissar. He stayed for only a few months and was replaced by another party man. His name was Trou Sho Ka, but he was commonly referred to as Trou Su Shi or Trou the Commissar. He was around thirty-five and a civilian, though he had previously served in the Red Army. He was a big, stocky man and a convinced and dedicated Communist. His self-effacing and gentle manner concealed a ruthless and devious personality. The Commissar was also a great advocate of the policy of "self-determination and self-rule." He held forth on this topic during meetings and always assured the Tibetan officials that the Chinese had no desire whatsoever to remain in Tibet.

"Tibet must be ruled by the Tibetans," he would say. "We Chinese are only here as guides to help you. In a year or two we will leave, and you will have to manage on your own. Even if you ask us to stay then, we will not do so."

It is a humiliating admission to make, but we really believed him. The behaviour of the Communist officers and soldiers was irreproachable. They conscientiously paid for all the supplies they bought and never used threats, except as a final resort. They wisely made no changes in the social and political hierarchy and they did not try to change a single one of our customs or traditions. They even pretended to have respect for our religion. We had no reason for doubting their intentions.

At the meetings in the Castle of the Female Dragon, Trou the Commissar repeatedly stated that the Tibetan administrators were to make the decisions. He maintained that his role was solely that of an adviser. Initially the Chinese did play it that way, but gradually they let us know who our real masters were. Of course, it was very subtly done, over a period of years. Many of us had suspicions and uneasy feelings, but these were allayed by the generosity, friendliness and the reasonable behaviour of the Chinese authorities. The Chinese were very eloquent and had a stock of ready-made answers to all our simple questions. The "advisers" would give more and more advice, they verbally dominated the meetings. They would skilfully counter decisions made by us Tibetans, and if we insisted, they would come up with that inevitably effective rejoinder:

"We understand it is very hard for you to see our point of view. You have not yet developed a political consciousness," Trou the Commissar would say earnestly. "You will learn these things in the future. You must accept the advice we are giving you as a genuine lesson in political thinking, and begin to act accordingly."

At the end of 1953, the Chinese completed the motor road to Kondo Trikhor, on the way from Derge to Chamdo. There was now no more need for people to transport supplies to Derge Yhilung. The Chinese decided to hold a big celebration to commemorate this event. It was held at Derge Yhilung and there was a very grand reception, hosted by the 18th Division. An army representative thanked the people for having hauled supplies and then awards of brocades and certificates drawn on red silk were distributed. Compensation was also paid to people whose pack animals had died or suffered injuries. The airfield at Kanze had also been completed at this time and the Chinese wanted to make a grand event of the landing of the first plane. A great banquet was held to impress the Tibetan dignitaries. It was the first plane we had ever seen, and if it was the intention of the Chinese to impress us with it, they succeeded.

In our sub-district of Wulu, our Chinese "adviser" was a person whom we knew as Shen the Commissar. He was also the chief assistant to Trou the Commissar. Shen was an old soldier and a member of the party. He had been twice wounded in the war with Japan and had a reputation for courage and integrity. He was about forty-five, and although he could be short-tempered at times, he was quite friendly to me. Our relationship was a strange one. He knew that nearly all Tibetans hated the Chinese, and that we secretly made rude jokes and comments about them. He must have realised our devotion to our religion and our antipathy to his cause. Yet his friendship was sincere and he did not discuss Marxist doctrines when speaking with us. He never gloated over the Chinese victories in Tibet, and this made him more than tolerable. As an old soldier, he must have known what defeat was like.

At the beginning of 1954, the Chinese called a general assembly of the people in the district and announced their plans for "economic change for the welfare of the people." Fallow land was to be provided for the landless and also for those whose holdings were small. To achieve this, a survey of all uncultivated land was made, and the Chinese promised to provide seeds and farming implements. Small groups of officials were sent to the surrounding villages to execute this plan. From our sub-district, Shen the Commissar and six other minor functionaries, including myself, were sent to the villages of Lakay to make arrangements for the distribution of fallow land.

The land was distributed with much ceremony and speech making, and everybody was made to clap heartily when the title deeds were handed over to the poor people. An official Chinese photographer ran around taking pictures and yelling at the interpreters to tell the stupid Tibetans to smile.

The programme for the distribution of fallow land was an unmitigated failure. First of all, agricultural land — that is, land in the valleys and close to a stream or another source of water — was already in use. The only sort of virgin land available was not close to any supply of water, or was up in the hills. Anyway, land alone never made a farmer, and the type of people to whom the Chinese distributed the land were professional beggars or the usual layabouts that are found in every village and town. All of them were horrified at the thought of doing some honest work, and most of them sold the free seeds and implements, and returned to their usual haunts to resume their drinking and carousing.

After completing our task, Shen the Commissar and I went to deliver our report to Commissar Trou. He listened to our detailed report and said, "I am pleased with your work but you have not yet fulfilled the most important part of your mission. You must try and locate those who are intimately associated with the people, who possess the power to alter public opinion and who have the trust of the people. It is also important to know how much gold, silver and cash each family has. These are extremely important tasks that have to be accomplished, but you must never discuss them openly."

When we came out of the office, I asked Shen what exactly Commissar Trou had in mind. He replied, "Commissar Trou has told you these things in strict confidence. Normally these matters are only discussed among Party members. He was referring to the introduction of democratic reforms. It is of paramount importance to recognise the people who have the ability to affect public opinion, and who are acknowledged by the masses as reliable men and leaders. Without such vital knowledge, we will never be able to introduce democratic reforms into the country. The first and quintessential step is to sever the bond between the masses and their traditional leaders, or the people they normally look to for guidance. Further steps are impossible without first accomplishing this. It can only be achieved in the guise of elevating the economic plight of the masses.

"We have great hope in you and therefore have taken you into our confidence. Hence you must do your best and prove yourself worthy of the trust we have placed in you. Only then can you ever call yourself a true Communist."

I was rather confused and puzzled by all this friendship and trust. I could plainly see that the Chinese did not mean well when they spoke of "economic reforms" or "self-determination." One could understand their use of hard persuasion when they wanted transport for army supplies to Derge Yhilung or for building the airfield at Kanze; it was a question of war and therefore necessary. We did not like it but we could understand the reasons behind those actions. But today's revelation gave me the first glimpse of the devious manouevres and intricate web of deception that the Chinese were preparing for us.

In 1954, the Chinese made one of their first moves to destroy the existing social structure. On the surface the changes were very innocent. The four chues or sub-districts were divided into hsiangs as called by the Chinese — Wuya, Manchu Khong, Yanche Khong, Lakay and also the town around the Female Dragon Castle. Nomads and their pasture lands were not included in these divisions. Each hsiang had

one head, the *hsiang tang*. There was also an assistant head, a
secretary and a captain from the People's Militia. All these
minor officials were appointed by the Chinese and were
carefully hand-picked. They were mostly the village riff-raff.
Some were from genuinely poor families, others those who
had grievances against their leaders. They were given generous salaries although they did not have much work to do.
Later, the administration of the hsiangs expanded and more
people were recruited into its service.

In 1955 we were sent on a publicity mission again to all the
villages in Wulu chue; this time to distribute free food and
clothing to the villagers in an attempt to win them over to
Communism. We were instructed to hammer home the slo-
gan "food for the starving, clothes for the naked and perfect
justice for all." But there was a catch. As each family received
its share of food and clothing, the head of the household had
to declare the amount of property and wealth that he possessed. The Chinese explained that this was being done only to
ensure the proper and fair distribution of free food and clothing.

The Chinese visited all homes and surreptitiously noted the
state of the family and the amount of gold, silver and grain it
possessed. They gave presents to members of the household
and made conversation. Direct questions about wealth and
status were not asked. Instead, innocent inquiries were made
about neighbours and the leading notables of the locality. The
villagers were naive and thought themselves clever for getting
free food and clothing from the Chinese in exchange for some
common information that was no real secret. In this manner
the Chinese managed to get an accurate and complete list of
all the prominent people in the district and the amount of
wealth in every household. They were very thorough. They
gave candies to small children and asked them questions about
their parents and elders.

In retrospect, it does seem surprising how easily the
Chinese managed to exploit our naivety and our only too
human greed. Their clever talk, presents and silver blinded us

while they drew a noose around our necks. It was too late when we remembered the old adage:

> Beware of the sweet honey
> Offered on the blade of a knife.

With the coming of Trou the Commissar, political lectures and self-criticism meetings were increased. The Communists considered these sessions their greatest weapon. Mao Tse Tung himself had commented at length on this insidious tool, and it held priority over all other activities. The basic self-criticism sessions were held in small committees, and members had to recount their mistakes and misdeeds for the week. Then everyone was obliged to accuse each other of whatever faults they possessed or whatever misdeeds they had committed. Even trivial quirks of personality and differences in behaviour were ferociously attacked and painfully dissected. The culprit was then severely remonstrated and exhorted to do better. Detailed records of all these sessions were kept and copies were routinely submitted to the *kung chou*, the secret police. These minutes were checked before each meeting to see whether wayward members were repenting or whether they were still indulging in their sins. If the culprit did not correct his behaviour to the satisfaction of the committee, he was denounced before a general assembly. If the person was still unrepentant, criminal charges were drawn up against him and he was sent for a spell in some "Thought Correction Centre," which in fact was a prison. If his crime was considered very serious, he was summarily executed.

To me, there was something indecent and repugnant about grown men accusing each other of taking an extra piece of Chinese steamed bread at lunch, or teasing a girl in the market place. When you confessed your misdeeds you really had to rack your brain to think of a misdemeanour convincing enough to suit everybody's morbid sensibilities, but not serious enough to get you into trouble. And then there were those really diligent characters who would always prowl around the edge of a conversation waiting to pounce on an indiscretion they could triumphantly expose to a shocked committee. Everybody spied on each other. Not even Trou the Commissar was immune to this, though he was very reticent. But it did achieve what the Communist leaders wanted: it kept all officials and citizens on their toes, it exposed those whose feelings opposed the regime and it created an atmosphere in which people could not trust one another. Thus it kept the dangers of a conspiracy to a minimum.

Anything that was a source of pleasure or fun for us was an excuse for a sermon. If a young man swaggered down the street in a new and dashing suit of clothes, the Chinese would not stop to admire him or even to laugh at his vanity. Instead they would moralize on the cost of the robes and how so many Chinese could be decently clothed for the price of that one rich robe. If people were singing and dancing, the Chinese would say they should be working. If a young man had an affair with a girl, they would act scandalized. Their songs were gloomy paeans dedicated to themes like "reconstruction" or the "four cardinal rules and the eight points of attention" or "The Great Helmsman Chairman Mao." We could barely tolerate much less sing about these and similar subjects. It seemed to me that the Communists just loved misery.

The tightening of Chinese rule did have one good though unintended benefit. It made people forget their past feuds and quarrels. Even Pachen put aside his old grudge and we became friends once again.

I was being granted less leave from my work and I constantly missed my wives and my little baby girl, born in 1950. I was careful never to complain, but people must have noticed my sadness, for at two self-criticism meetings I was accused of malingering and caring more for my family than the "Great Motherland."

7 "Learn from the Wisdom of Chairman Mao"

One day around the middle of 1955 I was summoned by Trou the Commissar. He offered me a cigarette and informed me that I had been granted a scholarship to study at the South-West School for National Minorities in Chengtu, China. I thanked him for the honour and politely refused his offer. I pointed out that my wives and child would have difficulties if I left them all alone.

"You do not realise what a marvellous opportunity this is," argued Trou impatiently. "You will now have the chance to study Marxism properly and also to brush up on your Chinese. This could mean a lot you know. Don't you want to be a member of the Party?"

I wanted to tell him what he could do with his scholarship and his party, but instead I replied, "It is a great honour, this scholarship, but I am just a stupid farmer and too old for such things. Could not a younger and more suitable man be found instead of me?"

"Nonsense," he snapped, leaning forward in his chair. "You are only forty. It is too late to change anything and besides, the course is only for one year. You can take a week's leave and make the necessary arrangements for your family." There was a note of finality in his voice so I did not argue any more. I rose to leave.

"By the way," he said, peering at some documents, "you will find other Tibetans in this school so you won't feel too lonely. Two other men from Nyarong will be going with you. They are Gyashing Tsethar and Kyoyee Sangay. I think you know them."

My family was horrified to learn that I was leaving. My wives and in fact most women in Nyarong were extremely hostile and suspicious of the Chinese. The Communists could fool the men with official ranks and presents, but not the women. They were much more realistic and hard-headed than we were. I did my best to console my family and made arrangements with some of my friends to help the women with the fields and herds. It broke my heart to leave my wives and little girl in such uncertain times. I took my daughter in my arms and kissed her goodbye.

I went up north to Kanze on horseback, and from there got a lift on a Chinese truck going to Dhartsedo. There I met the other two men who were also going to China. Gyashing Tsethar was Pachen's son and it was for him that Pachen had tried to get my second wife. He was a good-natured young man, now around thirty. I remembered him as a little boy, skipping and hopping on that long road to Lhasa. Kyoyee Sangay was from lower Nyarong, and the son of a big chieftain there. He was the same age as Gyashing Tsethar. Both of them were not too happy about going to China and they gloomily confided all their misgivings and fears about the Chinese.

From 1951 the Chinese had made it mandatory for every district to send at least fifty people annually to China for studies. They insisted the students should be young boys and girls. People protested as no one wanted to send their children. Some families even went bankrupt trying to pay someone to go to China in place of their sons and daughters. As well as Tibetans other "National Minorities" such as the Mongols, the Turks of Sinkiang, Lolos and others were compelled to send their children to China. The largest School for National Minorities was in Peking and the one at Chengtu was almost as big. Earlier the Chinese had set one up at Dhartsedo but it was closed down after a year.

From Dhartsedo we travelled by bus for an entire day. We

crossed the Holora Pass and then we were really in China. Green paddy fields sparkled in the sun and Chinese peasants wearing large straw hats toiled in the sluggish heat. Pigs wandered about everywhere, sometimes stopping our bus in the middle of the road. The smells were different. Though not unpleasant, they were not smells of juniper or cold winds, the smells of home. It was all very strange.

Chengtu was a large, crowded, noisy and dirty city. There were many cars and buses and numerous rickshaws. There must have been thousands of them with their bells tinkling and going in all directions. This was before the Reds really cracked down on everything.

There were a lot of shops selling all sorts of strange and wonderful things, restaurants and movie theatres which invariably screened propaganda films. There were large bustling tea houses where you could order a pot of weak tea and a plate of melon seeds for a few coppers. One could sit there the whole day listening to the old story-tellers. There were also brothels. I learned they were not as fancy as they used to be before the Reds came, but somehow they managed to function. Most of the girls there were the daughters of rich families that had been deprived of their land and wealth by the Communist authorities.

After a year, there was a sudden nationwide crackdown on all such activities. Nearly all the prostitutes in China were rounded up and shipped off to concentration camps where they probably died in the great famines of the sixties, if disease, overwork, malnutrition or a guard's bullet had not killed them already. Brothel owners and pimps were invariably shot; one bullet each in the back of the head.

The South-West School for National Minorities was in the suburbs and we went there by rickshaw. The school was a block of large concrete buildings — all new and standing three storeys high. Some of the buildings were still incomplete. There were about three thousand students: eight hundred to a thousand Tibetans, Lolos and other aboriginals from the southern parts of the Sino-Tibetan border. The remaining students were essentially Chinese although they somehow qualified as National Minorities.

The routine was a rigorous one. We woke at five a.m., then cleaned our rooms. From six to eight there were calisthenics followed by breakfast. Classes started at eight and carried on until twelve. Lunch was at the school canteen and from one to five there were discussion sessions. Dinner was at five and after that everybody had to play games, usually basketball, until seven. From seven until nine there were language classes. We Tibetans had to study Chinese. All the lights were switched off at ten p.m.

Every week there was a general meeting where we were exhorted by the principal to save grain, kill flies, destroy sparrows, resist imperialism, remember comrade Norman Bethune, learn the correct handling of contradictions among the people and whatever else the Party communique was at that moment. We also had a criticism session every Sunday.

There were about a hundred students in my class, which was divided into eight committees. Our instructor was a Chinese called Ka Tu Tang. His lessons were translated by a Tibetan and a Lolo interpreter. The first part of our syllabus was called The Great Motherland.

We learned how Communism was first introduced into China in 1921, under the leadership of Mao Tse Tung. We were also taught about the birth of the Red Army in 1927, and the war against the Japanese and the Nationalists. During World War II, we were told, China, helped by Russia, fought against the Axis Powers. The victory of the "workers and peasants army" in their great war against the Japanese was solely due to the brilliant leadership of Mao Tse Tung. It was also revealed to us that had it not been for Communist China the entire world would have been subjugated by the Axis powers.

We were solemnly assured that with the exception of a distant and insignificant country called America, Russia and China were the only two major powers. This America and the Nationalist Government had been allies during World War II, but when this war terminated and the civil war began, America could not help the Nationalists at all and Communism triumphed. That was the irrefutable evidence of America's position as a "paper tiger." There was even a derisive song called Paper Tiger that we had to learn. The rest of the world had been liberated by Russia and China, and had welcomed Communism with open arms. Then the instructor pointedly stated that it was only stupid and backward people like the Tibetans, the Lolos and the Turks of Sinkiang who did not welcome Communism with open arms and flowers. We were earnestly admonished to learn better.

It was all incredibly crude. We Tibetans had been cut off from the world, but everybody knew about the war and the atomic bomb. Although we did not know all the details and the battles that took place, we knew more than enough to realise that the Chinese were treating us as complete idiots. Saying that America was a small distant country was both audacious and mindboggling. There were American products all over China and Tibet. Enterprising traders had flooded Tibet with American Army surpluses like tents, flashlights, uniforms, boots and field rations. Even here in our classroom our instructor had a Parker pen clipped to his shirt pocket. The Communists themselves craved American products, and the only non-American thing they ever desired were Rolex watches. A Chinese would gladly give his right hand for a Rolex.

I knew quite a lot about the World War and tried to keep myself constantly informed about it. I was in Lhasa, on my second pilgrimage, when the atomic bomb was dropped on Japan and the war finally ended. So when we heard this version of the war and the novel description of the big powers, most of us howled with laughter. Our instructor was genuinely surprised at our reaction. I never really understood whether he believed implicitly in the rubbish that he taught us, or whether he was surprised that we barbarians were not so gullible after all. Most of the Chinese students never laughed or sniggered at our "history" lessons as we Tibetans and Lolos did. I don't think they were all that stupid. Maybe they believed ... maybe they just wanted to believe.

Then we had to study the Chinese Constitution. There were a hundred and six points that Ka Tu Tang diligently explained, one by one. We were encouraged to ask questions which we eagerly did. Some of us had noticed ominous discrepancies that we thought needed better explanation. The first article in the constitution went something like this: "The socialist country of China, under the leadership of the working class, and with the unity and the cooperation of the workers and peasants, is a People's Democratic Nation." Another article in this same constitution ran: "Under the principle of centralism, the people of China will proceed on the road of socialism." What we wanted to know was, who was really supposed to be the leader — the workers as stated in the first article, or the centre as stated in the other?

Our instructor said that there was no difference, and he told us that even Chairman Mao had said so. He explained that the system was like two sides of a spinning wheel. No one side was above or beneath the other. We insisted that there was a difference. The leadership of the workers or peasants would mean a democracy. On the other hand, rule from the "centre" would just mean the dictatorship of the Communist Party.

Our instructor stated impatiently that the differences were superficial, and that we were not capable of understanding the many existing explanations. He then gave his own interpretation of the two articles. "The people will travel on the road of democracy towards centralism, under the leadership of the Communist Party. Democratic centralism is the only road to socialism."

There were other discrepancies that we questioned, but we never received any satisfactory answers. After our lessons on the constitution, the whole class was taken for a holiday tour of Chungking. From Chengtu, we travelled overnight by train and arrived at Chungking station at dawn. The city was built on the side of a hill at the confluence of two rivers. The whole are was rather mountainous, unlike Chengtu, which was absolutely flat. We were received at a fine hostel and royally treated. We were taken to various factories, some of which were quite interesting. Chungking was a big industrial city and there were many factories and mills. We were given systematic tours of an iron and steel plant, an electrical equipment factory, a woollen and textile mill and a cigarette factory.

We were shown each factory and given a detailed explanation of its processes by the manager. Then followed a fine reception where refreshments were served. The managers would inevitably spout the Party line. "Under the heroic leadership of Chairman Mao and the Communist Party, we work here for the people of the Great Motherland ... this factory is one important factor in the reconstruction and progress of the nation."

At the steel plant, we were informed that some of the ore being used was from Eastern Tibet. We were also taken to a coal-mine, a day's journey by car from Chungking. Some of us were taken into the long, endless pits, which was a novel and claustrophobic experience. After a very grand reception, we chatted with one of the managers. He mentioned that the coal-mine employed about thirty thousand people. One of us asked him how much each labourer was paid. He appeared very flustered and assured us that the labourers had enough food to eat and clothes to wear, and were very happy and satisfied. This explanation made us suspicious and we questioned him further. Finally he told us that our instructor would answer the questions as he was unable to do so. We realized that it would be no use insisting and so gave up.

We were also taken to a zoo and to the famous Buddhist Temple of the Five Hundred Arhats. Although there were no worshippers or monks around the temple, it was in reasonably good condition. Our tour lasted for about five days and we returned to Chengtu. The railway system was very well organised, the trains were clean and always on time. Before every stop, an announcement was made over a p.a. system, stating the name of the station and how long the train would stop there. But there were very few travellers on board. The Communist authorities clearly liked their citizens to stay home and work.

For our next course we had an instructor called Nge Tu Ring who was supposed to enlighten us on the "policy for national minorities." There were about forty points in this policy, each of which he meticulously explained. The essence was: "Under the leadership of the great Chinese race, all the different nationalities have been entitled to racial equality, cultural preservation and private property."

One Tibetan man asked, "How can the different races be said to enjoy racial equality when the Chinese are supposed to be the leaders?" The instructor replied, "You could also say, 'with the aid of the Great Chinese Nationality,' as the Chinese are superior in the brotherhood of nationalities. Our superiority is not just a dogma we are imposing on you, it is a historical fact. The Chinese are the most culturally advanced pioneers of civilization. Take Chairman Mao for example, such cultured men are extremely rare in this world. There are many such advanced personalities among us Chinese and that is why we have become the leaders."

One Lolo boy got up and angrily remonstrated with the instructor. "Your conception of equality is a farce since you insist on the idea of one race being superior to the rest. I am a Lolo and proud of it — I do not think I am in any way inferior to a Chinese." We all cheered!

The Lolos were tribal people living in the southern borders of China and Tibet. They were proud people and mean fighters, fond of weapons and strong drink. The men wore big turbans on their heads and bedecked themselves with ornaments made of coral, conch shells and cowries. A Lolo admired a man only for his strength and courage. Racially, they were completely different from the Chinese, whom they despised. They revolted against the Chinese around 1955. It was a revolt of great magnitude and ferocity. The Lolos were reasonably well armed and operated in a terrain that was all jungle and craggy mountains. Their hatred of the Chinese was traditionally implacable, and it demonstrated itself very cruelly and savagely during the revolt. The Lolos never surrendered and they never took prisoners. Many Chinese divisions were rushed to the area and thousands of soldiers died in the subsequent fighting. Finally, through sheer weight of numbers and superior arms, the revolt was crushed. The reprisals were savage. Lolo men, women and children were bayonetted or shot in mass executions. The extent of these massacres will most probably never be known. What is known is that the Lolos have ceased to exist as a people.

Nge Tu Ring explained that the policy of nationalities had been approved by Mao Tse Tung and the Great National Assembly of China, and hence should be believed implicitly — without silly questions being asked by impertinent and foolish people.

We did persist in asking questions, but satisfactory answers were never given. Instead, another lecture was delivered on national customs and traditions. Nge Tu Ring explained that the customs and traditions of a nation should be divided into two categories: those that benefited society and which were to be preserved, and those that hindered the development of a country. He elaborated on this thesis giving special attention to us Tibetans. "The amount of food one Tibetan consumes is enough for three Chinese," he said, shaking his head disapprovingly. The Chinese students giggled. "Tibetans love to waste large quantities of food on lavish picnics and parties. I have heard that thousands of tons, yes, thousands of tons of butter are burnt in lamps every year, just as offerings in temples."

All the Chinese students stared at us and tried to look shocked. We were fuming with anger. "Their dances and songs are nice, but the words in their songs are totally reactionary. Yes," continued Nge Tu Ring, "and Tibetans have elaborate marriage ceremonies and love to affect expensive jewellery and ornaments which can neither satisfy one's hunger nor quench one's thirst. And they even have long hair which is not at all hygienic, and is also very reactionary. Are all these customs beneficial to society? No! Of course not."

Our instructor took special delight in attacking religion. "Although there is total freedom of religion in China, it is nevertheless the greatest obstacle hindering social advancement. Expensive and elaborate religious rites and ceremonies must be stopped. To counter the retrogressive effects of this poison, Chairman Mao is introducing certain reforms." He concluded by saying, "it is natural that when social reforms are introduced everywhere, all the different systems of administration, economy and culture will be amalgamated into a single unit. Then, and only then, will there be true socialism."

Nge Tu Ring had started the lesson with the premise that we were entitled to preserve our culture and traditions. But by now he had attacked practically all the salient features of our culture and religion, and had singled them out for ridicule and for what he called "inevitable reforms." He diligently tried to explain his points to us. "The culture and traditions belonging to your backward society must be reformed," he stated emphatically. "It is extremely important for you to push ahead through the right way prescribed by the great socialist system. A happy and prosperous life can only be attained by adopting socialism and following the unassailable leadership of Chairman Mao. Therefore, everybody must follow this path, this infallible system which has been introduced by Chairman Mao Tse Tung."

In the face of such absurdities and contradictions, we could not restrain ourselves and some of us started to argue heatedly with the instructor. "What is this talk of 'must'? Why must we follow any system laid down by Mao Tse Tung? You have just talked of 'racial equality' and the 'policy of national minorities.' What do you mean by all this, and your talk of freedom when you say that we 'must' follow your systems?"

Nge Tu Ring turned livid with rage and did not answer any of our questions. Instead he issued a grim warning, "Always remember that you have come here to learn from us, not to make policies. There is nothing surprising in what I have said.

The fact remains that you are a backward people and must be taught to do away with antiquated systems and adopt advanced ones. It is only when a country has undergone such a revolution that we can regard it as an advanced nation. Your very questions and impertinent arguments clearly illustrate how backward and old-fashioned your minds are. Learn from the Great People's Revolution — learn from the wisdom of Chairman Mao."

In the face of such dogmatic pig-headedness and irrationality there was nothing much we could do. The more questions we asked in class, the worse were the reprimands we received at the criticism sessions. Also, at the Sunday lectures, the principal would make pointed references to reactionary students. We learned that in the past critical students had been shipped to distant "Reform Through Labour" camps in order to "rectify" their thoughts. So little by little, we learned to keep our mouths shut and say just enough to please the instructors and keep the criticism sessions from becoming too boring.

Alone, amongst ourselves, we gave full vent to our feelings. All of us were terribly home-sick and hated this travesty of a school, but it opened our eyes to what the Chinese intended to do to us. I really learnt everything there was to know about Communism at that school — but not in the way that my instructors had ever intended.

"Democratic reforms" were introduced in 1956, in Eastern Tibet. This meant the total nationalisation of all private property and the formation of communes. "Democratic reforms" were also, in a way, the immediate reason for the great revolt in Eastern Tibet. The revolt had already started when we were in school, but we were kept totally ignorant of these developments. Instead we were told by our principal, "With the introduction of 'democratic reforms' the Tibetans are now enjoying social equality. When you students return to your native lands you will have to establish communes in your respective localities. This is the first step towards 'democratic reforms.' It is therefore imperative that you learn the fun-

damentals of establishing such communes." Our instructor
for this subject was Nge Tu Ring who had taught us "the
policy of national minorities." He once again subjected us to
his dreary dogma, monotonously delivered in his dry and
rasping voice.

"In a low class commune, the means of production, that is,
the land, herds, agricultural implements and seeds of every
individual, must be collected and retained by the commune,"
he began. "Each member will be permitted to retain other
personal items that are not 'the means of production.' But he
must, from this personal wealth, invest a fixed sum into the
commune.

Everyone will have to do his share of work, and at the end
of the year, after deducting taxes and seed reserves etc., each
member will be eligible for a share in fifty percent of the
harvest. This share will be based on each member's outlay in
'the means of production.' The rest of the harvest will be
equally distributed among all the members of the commune.
All individual incomes will be distributed in the form of
grains. This is not true socialism, as we are tacitly accepting
such anomalies as private land ownership. This only consti-
tutes a step towards true socialism.

"After a period of a year or two when things have progres-
sed more, the low class commune will be able to attain the
status of a high class commune. We are now getting to a stage
when Communism is taking root more deeply among the
people and the country. Now in the high class commune
there is no distribution of fifty percent of the harvest for
'means of production' outlay. Thus the question of private
ownership, the antithesis of socialism, is eradicated. The land,
herds, etc., all belong to the commune. In the high class
commune the individuals will be paid in the form of currency
notes on the basis of personal merit. This is real socialism.

"The amount of work completed daily will be judged
according to a points system. The most industrious labourers
will be awarded the ten points they deserve. Daily records
must be kept and the annual awards of currency must be in

accordance with the number of points the person has acquired. Also coupons must be issued, specifying the exact
amounts of grain that a person is entitled to buy. Local
granaries will be authorized to sell only a maximum of fifteen
kilograms of grain a month to a healthy adult worker. Others
will be entitled to smaller purchases in accordance with the
number of their points. Each person will not be permitted to
choose the grains, but must accept whatever grain is issued.
All labourers will be allowed to buy only half a kilo of butter
or oil monthly. In all cases, no supplies will be issued if a
worker fails to produce his identity card and food coupons."

We asked Nge Tu Ring if there was to be any consideration
for those who were either too old or too young to perform
manual labour. He declared that all those below sixty years of
age were capable of manual labour, while those beyond
seventy could still be used as human scarecrows to keep birds
off the fields.

When asked how the points of merit were to be given, and
their relationship to a person's daily income, he replied that
only officials and advanced people deserved the privileged
quota of fifteen kilos of grain per month. The most hard
working labourer would only receive about twelve kilos.
Older workers were to receive eight kilos, with five kilos for
children and two and a half kilos for infants. Thus, diligent
workers would generally get six to ten points a day, while
shepherds would only be eligible for four points. The human
scarecrows would receive only two points a day. Ten points a
day was equivalent to two R.M.P. (the official currency), and
a labourer would have to work for at least eight hours a day to
earn this. Nge Tu Ring elaborated further on the intricacies
and mysteries of the points sytems. "The income that the
government has fixed for the labourer is sufficient to make
ends meet, provided he does not indulge in extravagant picnics and parties. Chairman Mao has already initiated the 'new
economic system' called 'more production and less consump-
tion.' You must therefore start producing more and eating less
in order to improve the national economy. The only way of

advancing economically is by following this theme. Chairman Mao once said, 'How wonderful it would be if every Chinese could save a grain of rice at every meal. Each individual would thus be able to save three grains of rice daily, and the nation would accumulate eighteen hundred million grains of rice each day.' "

At this, we asked the instructor, "How can you expect your labourers to work hard when they do not get enough to eat? According to the system you have just explained, there will simply not be enough for a man to fill his stomach. Old people, cripples, the sick and children will have to suffer even more than the animals we kept before. In our land we may work our beasts in the day, but we let them eat as much as possible afterwards."

The instructor glibly replied, "It is the responsibility of the healthy worker to help his weaker counterpart. Everyone is capable of working. The crippled can stitch, the blind spin wool. Even children can perform simple tasks. Anyone who expects food without working is a parasite and an enemy of the people. We officials work with our minds, the workers must work with their bodies."

We persisted with our questions. "Do you mean to say that people who cannot work should be left to starve? What will happen to you when you grow old?" Nge Tu Ring was evasive and replied that we had misconstrued the meaning behind the policy of "democratic reforms," and that although everyone would have to work hard and make sacrifices for the present, a time would come when unbounded happiness and prosperity would prevail in the realm of the socialist system.

"When will we reach the socialist stage of unbounded happiness and prosperity?" we asked sceptically.

"When we come to the highest level in the development of the communes," he replied optimistically. "It will take about five years to reach the socialist stage. But to attain 'socialist utopia,' all the countries of the world will have to adopt Communism. You may expect this final stage to take place after the Third World War. You see, it is a matter of historical inevitability. This progress is slow but absolutely certain. This development can even be proved. Before World War I there was not a single socialist state. But Soviet Russia emerged from that war. Then after World War II, China and many other countries embraced Communism. It is only common sense to realize that after the Third World War, the whole world will embrace socialism. After that there will be no more wars and no more governments. Even the Communist Party will be disbanded and we will live in a world of peace and plenty."

There were many other lessons we were taught but I will mention them no further. Most of them were in the same vein as I have narrated, spiced with a lot of high sounding but empty slogans and an abundance of outright lies. We listened to the inconsistencies, contradictions and dogmas, and all the while counted the hours and the days when we would be allowed to leave for home.

Finally, after a year, in the fourth moon of 1956, we were informed that we had successfully completed our course and we were all awarded degrees.

I knew that matters would not be all that pleasant at home, yet a great happiness swept over me as I realised I was finally done with the school, and I would soon be seeing my wives and my little girl.

8 "Reforms" and Revolt!

At the beginning of 1956, the people of Nyarong and Eastern Tibet rose up in a great revolt. Throughout history our people have hated the Chinese, and it was on this rich soil of traditional animosity that the seeds of the revolt were first planted. The Reds had in the beginning pursued a deceptively mild course of action in Tibet — they paid handsomely for all supplies, they simulated respect for religion and the traditional social system, they played on the greed of the people with silver and honours and, above all, they glibly promised to leave as soon as Tibet was capable of self-government.

But as the years went by and the Reds gained in strength and confidence, they gradually tightened the screws on the country and began to introduce their "reforms." They did face a certain amount of opposition from the people, but it was sporadic, and by deception, lavish gifts, veiled threats and insinuations they succeeded in implementing their designs. But when the Chinese began to introduce a new programme called "democratic reforms" in 1956, they unexpectedly ran into a wave of spontaneous and violent opposition. All the repressed bitterness, hatred and misery of the Tibetans expressed itself in such a furious desire for vengeance that it initially surprised and confounded the Chinese.

"Democratic reforms" was the rather misleading term that the Chinese used for their grand design to eradicate the entire traditional social system, customs and religion, and to replace it with sterile communes rigidly controlled by hand-picked Party men. It was intended to sound the death-knell of our religion and the end of the Tibetans as a distinct race and nation.

In Nyarong, the Chinese had put their plans into action by increasing the personnel of the hsiangs, the local administrations. They had recruited layabouts and malcontents whom they used to denounce traditional leaders, lamas, scholars and people of importance. The Chinese had kept precise records of all prominent men in Nyarong and they now proceeded to move against them. The collaborators who were to do the dirty work were given the title of "the diligent ones" and were granted special privileges and cash awards. But many of them, despite their proletarian backgrounds, refused to co-operate with the Chinese. Undaunted, the Chinese officials, backed by the army, began to implement "democratic reforms."

Nyarong was introduced to these "reforms" with a horrifying display of Chinese brutality and ingenuity. Companies of Chinese soldiers accompanied by civil officials and "diligent ones" proceeded from village to village, demanding the surrender of weapons. They then held *thamzings* — so-called "struggle sessions" where village headmen, lamas and prominent citizens were denounced, beaten, humiliated and sometimes killed. The whole land was rocked by these events, and any last illusion of compromise or peace was shattered when the Chinese turned against the tribal leaders whom they had so far honoured and feted.

Gyurme of the Gyara Chipa family was our tribal chieftain and the Chinese-appointed administrator for our sub-district of Wulu chue. He was away on some business at Dhartsedo when a number of Chinese soldiers and an official came to his house, which was just two hours journey from the Castle of the Female Dragon. Gyurme's mother, his wife, his young son and an old family retainer were accosted by the Chinese who demanded that they surrender their weapons. The members of the family protested and the old lady declared they had none. Without another word, not even a single warning, the Chinese shot every one of them dead. This cruel and senseless murder enraged the people of Nyarong and the flames of the impending revolt now started to rage.

The actual revolt began on the fourteenth day of the first moon in 1956, at Upper Nyarong. The Gyari Tsang family were traditionally the chieftains of that area. Gyari Nima, the chieftain and his elder wife were away at Dhartsedo. Nima's younger wife, a beautiful and fearless woman, Dorjee Yudon, was left at home to look after family affairs. As the course of events drew to that one unavoidable conclusion, she made the decision that launched the revolt.

Dorjee Yudon gathered her men and weapons and despatched missives all over Eastern Tibet, urging the people to rise against the Chinese. Dressed in a man's robe and with a pistol strapped to her side, she rode before her warriors to do battle with the enemy. She ferociously attacked Chinese columns and outposts everywhere in Nyarong. The remaining Chinese soldiers and officials retreated to the Female Dragon.

The castle was stormed, with Dorjee Yudon herself leading the many charges. But the great walls of that old castle were built to withstand such attacks, and without artillery (which the rebels did not have) they were virtually impregnable. Casualties soared. Finally Dorjee Yudon decided to lay siege to the castle.

By now the whole countryside was in ferment and many other villages and tribes rose up to fight. Dorjee Yudon's task at the castle was proving to be difficult. The Chinese garrison was well stocked with food and ammunition, and they also had a spring of clear water within the walls.

After a month, six hundred troops from the 18th Division arrived from Kanze to relieve their beleaguered comrades in the castle. Dorjee Yudon met them at Upper Nyarong and managed to defeat them. About four hundred Chinese soldiers were killed, but two hundred managed to break through the siege lines and enter the castle.

Another column of about fifteen to twenty thousand soldiers poured in from Drango and Thau in the east. Dorjee Yudon was forced to give way and the siege was lifted. Yet the fighting accelerated and lasted for a month, after which the superior numbers and arms of the Chinese began to tell.

The Chinese suffered heavy losses, about two thousand dead and many more wounded. Two hundred officers were killed and their bodies were buried with much ceremony outside the old castle.

Finally the Chinese regained some measure of control in the country, and the rebels had to take to the hills from where they initiated a relentless guerrilla campaign. Day by day their numbers swelled.

After completing my studies at the School for National Minorities at Chengtu, I was permitted to leave for home. At Dhartsedo, the big trading centre and also the official head-quarters for the whole of Eastern Tibet, I and the other students were welcomed by the half-breed (Tibetan-Chinese) chairman of the Autonomous Area of Dhartsedo. He was called Sala the Chairman. He congratulated us on getting our degrees and gave us a long talk on recent events.

"Now that you have finished your studies, we accept you as advanced persons. This year we have introduced 'democratic reforms' and have liberated all the people in the areas under our jurisdiction. True, we have met with some opposition and resistance, instigated by reactionaries, but we have now managed to control the situation. It is your duty to maintain peace in your districts and oppose the anarchic activities of the rebels. Chairman Mao and the Communist Party have proposed a special policy called "the peaceful suppression of rebels." Any rebel who surrenders to the authorities will not be killed, imprisoned, or punished in any way and there will be no criminal charges brought against him. Aside from surrendering his weapons, he will be allowed to retain all his personal properties. No investigations will be made into his previous crimes against the people, and he will be permitted to live as peacefully as any other citizen in the country.

"People who surrender voluntarily will be rewarded with presents and honours. Rewards will also be given to any person who can persuade any rebel to surrender. This policy is a final one and will in no way be altered, regardless of what may happen."

This was an amazing about-face! The sheer audacity of this proclamation was a mockery and an insult to the intelligence of every Tibetan. None of us entertained the slightest belief in the value of this new policy. We were made to study it in depth for three days and to hold discussions on it. It was confidentially revealed to us that if we successfully managed to propagate this policy, we would be amply rewarded.

There were many eminent leaders and prominent citizens of Eastern Tibet in Dhartsedo at that time. They had been summoned ostensibly for official purposes, but in reality they were hostages. The Chinese had not arrested or imprisoned them, but they had been detained under the pretext of endless meetings and official work. The revolt had by now spread all over Eastern Tibet, and it was to the advantage of the Chinese to keep these leaders under their watchful eyes.

There was Chagoe Topden, one of the most important chieftains of Derge; Khangsar Yedoe of Kanze, Chanzoe Yeshe Dorjee of Drango, Mawo Chanzoe, a shrewd monk official from Thau and another monk official from the monastery of Sangre, in Lithang. From Linka She there was Gyakpon Chinee Dorjee and Gya Yonten. There were other chieftains besides and Tenzin Dhakpa (my brother-in-law) from Nyarong.

I secretly managed to meet a number of these people and also my brother-in-law. It was then that I learnt what had happened while I was away. I talked with these leaders and we exchanged ideas and opinions on how we could effectively fight the Chinese. But there were too many spies and informers in the town and it was difficult for all of us to meet inconspicuously in order to work out a joint plan of action.

We arrived in Nyarong towards the end of the fifth moon of 1956. Most of the able-bodied men had taken to the hills as guerrillas. The Chinese in their turn were retaliating by carrying out savage reprisals upon those left behind. Consequently I was detained at the Castle of the Female Dragon for a few days and not permitted to visit my home. The old fort was scarred and pock-marked with the bullets of the recent battles. My heart was heavy with sorrow and anxiety as I walked through the ancient gates and reported my arrival to Trou the Commissar. He had aged, but his hands were still steady as he lit his cigarette. He welcomed me and congratulated me on my successful graduation. "We have introduced 'democratic reforms' in Nyarong," he began, "and liberated the people. There have been some unpleasant incidents, but we have succeeded in establishing peace and order. Some of the reactionaries are still trying to hide in the mountains, but sooner or later they will all fall into our hands. Now you may visit your home, but make sure that you report back to headquarters after three days. By the way, I have a high opinion of your family, since they voluntarily distributed your land and grains to the people."

When I arrived, my wives and relatives were astonished to see me as they believed I had been murdered by the Chinese. Life during my absence had proved to be extremely frightening and difficult, and they wept as they told me what had happened. The Chinese had branded my family as "serf owners" and had confiscated nearly all my property — my entire reserve of grain, my herds, horses and even my wives' jewellery. Our family possessed a large copper pot, large enough to make tea for two hundred people and we had used it whenever a large congregation of monks came to our house, or whenever we had a large feast. The Chinese had also taken this away. Even a quilt that I had purchased from the Chinese co-operative store had been confiscated. Since the harvest had been bad that year, my family had borrowed about five sacks of grain from friends. The Chinese, when confiscating all our possessions, had coolly informed my wives that due to the beneficient foresight of the "People's Government," all loans were void and they would not have to pay back the creditors. Nevertheless, we did pay our friends back later.

We realised that this was only the beginning of our trials. My wives wanted us to flee. Our neighbours had their own tales of similar outrageous treatment and other miseries and hardships that they had suffered during the recent "reforms."

As I had been granted leave for only three days, I returned to headquarters on the fourth day, my heart weighed down with sorrow and apprehension.

After my arrival at the castle, I managed to meet some of the leaders of Nyarong and we confided our misgivings to each other and tried to find a way to a better future for our people. Of those I met, one was Nima of the Gyari Tsang family, another was Kyou Aben of the Gyongba Tsang family, chieftain of Lower Nyarong. There was also Sonam Wangchen, a deputy chieftain of the western nomads. All of us were at the castle at the behest of the Chinese authorities who wanted us to get the guerrillas to surrender. We were also instructed to go on publicity tours to convince the people that the Chinese were their saviours and that they should not have anything to do with the rebellion. But we had different ideas and we exchanged them at secret meetings.

Gyari Nima voiced our convictions: "I can no longer live under the Chinese," he declared, "it is my belief that we should all revolt and overthrow their hated rule. If we are ever to achieve this, then the entire population of Nyarong must unite to form an effective resistance force to fight the Chinese." We sent secret messages to all the other leaders informing them of our decision and urging them to unite and resist the Chinese.

During my stay at the castle, I happened to come across Shen the Commissar. I asked why my family had been branded as "serf owners" when we were nothing of the sort. He replied that I had studied Communism and the reason should be apparent to me. I was not satisfied with this vague explanation and began to argue with him. "I am no big landlord or rich man. You know I have been borrowing grain this last year. What are all these accusations for?"

"All right, I'll give you your answer," Shen replied reluctantly. "I was not exactly avoiding the issue when I told you that the reasons should be apparent. You know, we have to watch those people who have qualities of leadership, or those that the masses look to for guidance. This is Party policy. In order to disillusion the people about their reactionary leaders, we expose them as serf owners, thus revealing their true and ugly faces behind the masks. Of course, not all these people are really serf owners. Some of them might be as poor as the rest of the people. But that is only a technicality as the thoughts of all these people are reactionary and feudal. If they had the opportunity they would undoubtedly become serf owners. You are one of them. So learn and mend your ways."

The area of Thangkya in eastern Nyarong was in guerrilla hands. All the population of the three valleys that formed Thangkya and the nomads of neighbouring Phisa were actively hostile to the Chinese, and they supported and supplied the guerillas. No Chinese could pass through the area. The Chinese launched a "peaceful suppression of rebels" campaign in that district, and two thousand crack troops of the 3899 regiment under General Shao were sent to implement this campaign. Gyashing Tsethar (who had been with me in China) and I were to accompany this force. Two prominent lamas, Pema Tenzin and Ngudup were also to join us. We four Tibetans were to do our best to persuade the guerrillas to surrender.

On our arrival at Thangkya, we were kept close to the General and were constantly surrounded by a ring of guards, who accompanied us everywhere on the pretext of protecting us from guerrillas. Our task in "suppressing the reactionaries" was to make announcements denouncing the guerrillas, warning people not to help them and praising "democratic reforms." We were also made to write letters to the guerrillas assuring them that there would be no reprisals and punishments if they surrendered and accepted Communist rule.

Word reached the Chinese forces that three nomad families had been sighted at the Thangkya pass. Most probably, the report ran, they were guerrillas. A detachment of two hundred soldiers under Colonel Len was dispatched to capture them. It was dusk when they rode out and they returned the next day with the news that the guerrillas had already fled.

Len the Colonel was a friendly person and he often chatted with us Tibetans, especially at meal-times, as he liked to eat with us. On his return from the pass, he was describing the trip when he made a comment that revealed the extent of Chinese intentions.

"... and of course, when we got there, there was nobody, and a good thing for them too ... otherwise we would have wiped out every single one of them."

We were shocked upon hearing this and Lama Pema Tenzin asked him whether it was Communist policy to execute innocent people, even women and children.

"No, of course not," the Colonel replied. "But these people are rebels. And as far as rebels are concerned, our instructions are very clear. We are to exterminate them all, even the women and children. I mean, who will feed the women and children anyway? It is better that they die. Little rebel children will grow up and make trouble in the future. If you squash the nits, there will be no more lice. These were the orders given to me by the General. Anyhow, this talk is between us only, so don't go around repeating it."

Since recent events, we never really had any doubt about Chinese intentions. But hearing it so plainly and casually from the mouth of a rather friendly officer, drove in with force the dreadful and frightening truth that our minds had not, until that moment, fully grasped. I now realised there could be no forgiveness, no compromises, not even the least accommodation on both sides. We had to fight them and kill them, no matter how impossible it was to win, because they were going to destroy us anyway.

All the inhabitants of Thangkya were rounded up for a mass meeting. Addressing them, Shao the General announced: "Now that we have introduced democratic reforms you have been fully liberated. There will be no one to suppress you or take away your land and property. We will provide for those who do not possess land for cultivation. We are here to help you all."

The General's speech was followed by those of two other Chinese officials, after which we also had to make speeches. The people were then asked if they had anything to say. No one uttered a single word. The General was rather irritated at this silence and shouted: "Now that we have granted you freedom of speech, make use of it. You need have no fear." He repeated this several times and finally an old man rose from the crowd. He was dressed in faded and patched robes and his boots had evidently seen better days. But he stood tall and upright, his dark eyes bright with ill-concealed hostility and indignation.

"My name is Shanam Ma," he declared in a clear and proud voice, "I am a poor man and an old one, as you all can see. There are a few things that have to be said here today and it is best that I say them. Since I am poor, I have nothing to lose; since I am old, death will come soon anyway. I have this to say to you Chinese. Ever since you entered our land, we have barely been able to tolerate your behaviour. Now you try to force some strange new "democratic reforms" on us that we all think are ridiculous and nothing but a mule load of conceit. What do you mean you will give us land, when all the land you can see around you has been ours since the beginning of time? Our ancestors gave it to us, and you cannot give it to us again. If there is anyone oppressing us it is none other than you. Who has given you the right to force your way into our country and push your irrational ideas onto us? We are Tibetans and you are Chinese. Go back to your homes and to your people. We do not need you here."

Another man, Apel Tsultrim, rose and spoke in a similar manner and the people roared their approval. The Chinese quickly concluded the meeting.

The following night, General Shao summoned the Chinese officials and the four of us to his tent. He declared that the old man Shanam Ma and Apel Tsultrim were "serf owners" and ordered their arrest. That same night the General received a reply from the guerrillas in response to the letters that we had been ordered to write to them. I read it to the General and the officers. "To the chieftains and the sub-chieftains of the Chinese bandits," the letter ran. "We do not ask for mercy, nor do we negotiate with thieves and bandits who ride into our homes, murder our people and steal our lands and wealth. We deal with such villains in only one way — with swords and guns. Go home, go home now, when your lives are still intact in your bodies, for if you continue to oppress us we will surely split them asunder."

The General was furious. He stamped his feet and screamed in indignation: "We will annihilate them. They are just reactionary fools." After a time, he calmed down somewhat and declared, "I will give them one last chance to surrender." We were then ordered to write to the guerrillas again. The General promised us that if we could get so much as one guerrilla to surrender we would be handsomely rewarded.

But the guerrillas only sent ruder replies and stepped up their activities. The General sent many patrols and detachments to trap them, but most of his soldiers never returned. The Chinese soldiers were no match for the guerrillas. They knew nothing of the terrain and were slaughtered in cunning and fatal ambushes. Finally, casualties rose so high that the General was forced to keep his troops on the defensive and the guerrillas had a free run of the area again. But to save face, General Shao spread the word that he was slowly but surely gaining the upper hand.

On the night when the old man Shanam Ma and Apel Tsultrim were arrested, Chinese officials were despatched to the surrounding villages to find evidence that the two of them were serf owners, and also to find people who would denounce them. The officials returned with four poor beggars, but reported that they could not dig up any evidence that the two prisoners were serf owners. The General was not in the least perturbed by this and declared that if they were not serf owners, they must at least be in league with the rebels.

He ordered all the people in the area to be summoned to a meeting. The four beggars were given a good meal, and as soon as the people had assembled, Shanam Ma and Apel Tsultrim were brought out in chains. Addressing the four beggars, the General said, "You four are advanced people. These two men in front of you are in league with the rebels and should be purged of their evil and anti-social ideas. Therefore, tell the people of the crimes of these two reactionaries. Denounce them."

But the four beggars replied, "The two accused men are poor like ourselves and we do not know of any crimes they have committed. Please excuse us from this duty. We are poor and simple folk and know nothing of such matters." Infuriated at this unexpected response, General Shao dropped all pretence of legality and justice, and abused and spat at the four frightened beggars. "You fools, are you also the dupes of the reactionaries and feudal lords? Are you sympathisers of these blood-sucking rebels? Only your denunciations can prove your innocence. Do you understand?" The General paused for breath and wiped his face with a large handkerchief. "However, you need not fear the rebels, we will always protect you." But the beggars shuffled their feet and became frightened and confused. Finally the General summoned some soldiers and made them raise their rifles. Thus compelled, the four beggars made a faltering denunciation of Shanam Ma and Apel Tsultrim. Aided by the soldiers the four beggars were then made to beat the two prisoners. Both of them were barely alive when the meeting was finally terminated. Shocked and terror-stricken at this example of Chinese ruthlessness, the people were further informed by the General that such would be the fate meted out to all rebels.

For their part in this tragic affair, the four beggars were given, in public, a reward of a hundred silver dollars each, four rifles and ammunition. General Shao made a short speech at the presentation and praised them as true "model citizens" of the new China. Three days later however, two of the "model citizens" fled with their new rifles and joined the guerrillas, and the others were made to give up their guns.

We stayed with the soldiers for about four months, and

although fraternization was frowned upon and there were informers and spies everywhere, we did manage to talk to a lot of soldiers and learn about their hard and unhappy lives. They had been recruited from various provinces of China. When they had first enlisted, their heads had been shaved and they had to keep them that way. For three years they were not granted any leave nor were they permitted to marry or consort with women. Even after three years the soldiers had to apply for permission to marry. This application was forwarded to some office in Peking. After a long time, if the soldier concerned was lucky, permission might finally come. They were not permitted to drink alcohol or to save money. Any infringement of these rules was dealt with immediately and severely. Their behaviour towards civilians was strictly regulated by a code of conduct called "The Three Cardinal Rules and the Eight Points for Attention," which they had to memorise. A heroic tune had been composed for it and the soldiers had to sing it when they marched. They received just enough money to buy toilet goods and a few cheap cigarettes. The men dressed in drab, shapeless khaki uniforms while the officers, at that time, affected Russian style uniforms with large yellow and red epaulettes. When they were not at war or in training, the soldiers were constantly made to work digging ditches, hauling manure and so on.

They were never given a free moment and were subjected to endless criticism sessions to weed out slackers and malcontents. Informers and spies constantly roamed the ranks and every soldier was forced to live within a lonely shell of suspicion and mistrust. It was a deliberate and callous policy of the Communist High Command to thus subject their own soldiers to such a miserable life. Battle came as a relief to such tormented and weary men and the brutality and hardships of the battle field seemed normal to them. Since they had no wives to return to, no property, nothing to call their own, even death did not hold its usual terror and apprehension. Their officers cared not a whit for the lives of the soldiers and sent them on blind frontal assaults, regardless of casualties.

The officers themselves remained in the rear with pistols or sub-machine guns to ensure that no soldier turned back. It was all very sad and shameful and made war a far more grim and implacable sort of business than it had ever been.

In the whole of Eastern Tibet, there were about a hundred thousand troops. They were armed with various types of rifles, though these were later replaced by a standard Russian pattern semi-automatic rifle, the *Bura*. They also had Russian sub-machine guns and hand grenades. On the heavy side, they had machine-guns, mortars and howitzers, and mountain guns that could be taken to pieces and hauled on the back of mules. No tanks or armoured cars were used in Eastern Tibet, as the terrain did not permit it. But they had bombers based at Chengtu that caused us a lot of discomfort later.

We were ordered back to the castle after four months. The guerrilla bands were still operating with relentless fury and the Chinese policy of "peaceful suppression of rebels," though widely propagated, proved to be quite ineffective. One incident took place at that time that tragically exposed the inherent treachery of Chinese promises and effectively destroyed any remaining illusions about the policy of "peaceful suppression of rebels."

Sanag Palden was the leader of a large guerrilla band, and although the Chinese had made many attempts to capture and destroy him, they had never succeeded. Finally, the Chinese discovered that he was a faithful disciple of the Lama Tsewang Gyurme, a hermit who lived far away in the mountains. They arrested the old man and then sent a message to Sanag Palden informing him that the life of his Lama depended on his surrender. The Chinese also promised to abide by all the conditions in the policy of "peaceful suppression of rebels." Sanag Palden left his men in the mountains and gave himself up. He was arrested and summarily executed. The Chinese then announced that Sanag Palden's surrender was not genuine. They claimed that he had given himself up in order to spy on the Chinese.

At the end of that year, a "fact-finding and condolence

mission" was sent from Peking to placate the hostile people of Eastern Tibet and other "national minorities" (like the Lolos) who had revolted against Chinese rule. This mission based itself at Dhartsedo, and was composed of important Chinese leaders, including Wang Lo, a member of the Central Committee of the Communist Party and also the Chairman of the National Minorities Commission. From Dhartsedo, many delegations were dispatched to the various regions where people had revolted. The delegations that came to Nyarong consisted of a senior officer of the secret police, Kung An Chou, a senior PLA officer from Peking, some other Chinese officials and a few Tibetans. A large meeting was called and all the Tibetan leaders, prominent citizens and religious dignitaries — at least those who had not yet taken to the mountains — were invited to attend. The members of the delegation expressed their "heartfelt sorrow" for the troubles that the people had to face because of the "mistakes" of the local officials. They expressed their ideas in a long speech.

"Democratic Reforms should have been implemented gradually, bearing in mind the policy of 'peaceful methods and the gentle path.' Yet the regional officials have misunderstood their instructions and have caused all this sorrow and hardship to the people. Chairman Mao has expressly sent us to console those of you who have suffered so much for official blunders. As a token of our sincerity, we wish to distribute gifts of food and clothing to the people. All this is the fault of the local Chinese officials. Their mistakes are criminal offences against the people." The delegation admonished and castigated Trou the Commissar, who silently endured it all and did not seem to be in the least bit perturbed. The Police officer of our region was a Chinese whom we knew as Captain Kao. He was also reprimanded by the mission, but he denied all the charges and asserted that he had made no mistakes and had only followed instructions from Peking.

Large consignments of grain and textiles were brought from China and distributed among the people. The chieftains and other leaders received bolts of silk and brocade amongst many other fine presents. The "fact finding and condolence mission" stayed for a month, during which all the "reforms" and thamzings came to a halt. A new "liberalization policy" was announced for the whole of Eastern Tibet. After the delegation left, matters gradually became worse again and the Chinese officials soon recommenced forcing all their programmes and "reforms" down the throats of the people.

I was rather confused by this elaborate farce and confided my thoughts to a young Chinese officer who was friendly to me. He explained the situation and was unusually frank and bitter as he spoke.

"This blunder is not a mistake of local officials but the deliberate work of the government and the Party in Peking," he admitted sadly. "Premier Liu Shao Chi wanted to apply reforms with the policy of peaceful methods and the gentle path, but Chairman Mao has declared that this was a tardy way to socialism and has instead advocated the policy of peaceful methods and militant path to implement reforms. I myself prefer Premier Liu Shao Chi's ideas, but we are forced to obey Chairman Mao's orders as his power is now greater and Liu Shao Chi will soon be purged. But even if Liu Shao Chi came to power we would suffer, as we have, in a way, backed Chairman Mao. For us small officials it is always a dangerous world.

"According to our ideology, wisdom can be divided into sincerity and education, of which sincerity is the most important. Even when a man makes a mistake, the Party should judge whether the mistake was sincere or deliberate. A sincere mistake can be forgiven, while deliberate wrongdoings must be punished. But this ideology and sincerity have no place in the rivalry between leaders in Peking."

At this time, a special office was set up at the Castle called "The Political Deliberation Committee." All the available chieftains, lamas and other leaders were made to attend its meetings and lectures. Most of them were thus obliged to live at the castle where the Chinese could keep a sharp eye on them. The Chinese were very eager to start communes and I was instructed to start two communes in our sub-district of Wulu chue. I protested, but the Chinese were adamant, so finally a compromise was reached where the communes would only be experimental ones. Seeds, implements and animals would be provided by the Chinese and rations would be issued to all members for the first year. It was to be run in a modified way so there would be no "point system" and everyone would reap equal benefits whether he was old or young and healthy. It was not very successful. The people were unhappy with this new form of life and missed their freedom and the right to own property.

In the fourth moon of 1957, Gyari Nima, the Chieftain of Upper Nyarong (and the Chinese-appointed Chief Administrator of Nyarong) joined the guerrillas and sent us a message advising us to do the same. Though we were eager to comply, matters were complicated by the fact that we were always under the close scrutiny of the Chinese. We made careful plans for our escape, but just as we were about to leave, the Chinese called a meeting of all the sub-district administrators and the people's representatives of Nyarong.

Being one of the representatives, I was compelled to attend the meeting and postpone my earlier plans. At the meeting I had to make a report on the progress of the Experimental Lower Class Communes. Some of the more outspoken delegates asked me very tricky questions, casting some very revealing doubts about the Chinese motivation behind the whole commune system. I could not give them an honest answer, as that would have drawn too much attention to my real feelings, but I managed to make my points sufficiently well to placate the delegates and not arouse Chinese suspicion.

There were about one hundred and fifty delegates at the meeting and Trou the Commissar nominated Da Tse Cha, another Chinese official for the post of Chief Administrator. However, as the delegates did not show too much enthusiasm for this proposal, Trou the Commissar announced that since the actual appointment was to be decided the next day, everyone should think carefully and come to a decision by then. That very evening, Chinese officials met all the delegates individually and advised them to back Commissar Trou's candidate. So the next day, everyone raised hands in unanimous support of the Commissar's nomination and Da Tse Cha was elected as the new Chief Administrator of Nyarong. We later learnt that Da Tse Cha had already been appointed at Dhartsedo by the Chairman of the Autonomous Area of Dhartsedo, and that our election had been a mere farce. All the delegates were extremely angry.

Similarly in other meetings, all decisions were passed either directly or indirectly by the Chinese themselves. Our part in these affairs was to serve as puppets, to be manipulated at will by the Chinese.

Once again we were ordered to accompany the Chinese soldiers, who this time were heading for Lag Ri Ma, an area east of Nyarong whose inhabitants were nomads. Food and clothing were distributed to the people there and they were assured that no reforms or class struggles of any kind would be introduced if they did not desire them. At the same time, the Chinese secretly began to conduct a thorough investigation of the material conditions of each nomad family.

Then suddenly one day about a thousand Chinese soldiers marched into the area. Taken by surprise, the nomads were surrounded and their weapons seized. In the confusion, about forty nomads managed to break through the encirclement and take refuge in the high mountains. Of those left behind, fifteen were selected as "potential diligent ones" to receive special "thought rectification" education. These fifteen were granted certain privileges and were provided with arms and ammunition as an incentive and example of Chinese goodwill.

A couple of days later, however, six of the "potenial diligent ones" fled, taking their newly acquired weapons with them and joined those who had earlier managed to escape. The remaining "potential diligent ones" were summoned by the Chinese and relieved of their ammunition except for five cartridges each. At this stage I was sent back to the castle with some reports that I was to deliver to the Chief Administrator.

There were many other incidents of Chinese injustice and heavy-handedness that gradually gave even gentle and simple folk no choice but to revolt. I was once sent to buy butter for the Chinese and was instructed to trade grain and other things in exchange. Normally the nomads sold cheese, curds and other dairy products besides butter. But the Chinese insisted on a strict deal, whereby they demanded only a large quota of butter that the nomads could not possibly supply. An exasperated nomad shouted at us, "Even if I collect all the dung in the region and give it to you instead of butter, I will not be able to fulfil your demand."

The Chinese never hesitated to go back on their previous statements if it served their purpose. Thus Party communiques and instructions from Peking were constantly changing, and even local officials were confused when a new order from Peking totally contradicted previous instructions. A good example of this was the changes in the party communiques from 1956 to 1958 on the question of class struggle. Prior to 1956, the Chinese had declared that there would be no class struggle. The change began from 1956.

> ... The unending class struggle between serfs and landlords must be a peaceful one.

> ... The class struggle between serfs and landlords must be an open one, though it must be peaceful and only verbal.

> ... The people must "throw their tears of misery" on the landlords, and must begin an unending struggle until feudalism is wiped out.

> ... All landlords are the enemies of the people. They are like rotten meat. If we do not destroy the meat, it will always smell and collect flies.

After this all pretences were dropped.

I undertook my last mission for the Chinese at the beginning of 1958. A deposit of copper ore had been discovered in western Nyarong, at the hill of Wari Go, in the sub-district of Kholo Shi. I had been to this place before the invasion, and had noticed that the rocks and soil around this area were of an unusually reddish colour. Anyway, two Chinese surveyors and geologists arrived from Dhartsedo and I was ordered to accompany them to the site of the deposit. The Chinese geologists seemed extremely elated at the discovery and told us that this was an unusually large deposit. After they had returned to China, engineers and other people came to build a road to the site. Their plan was to link Wari Go with Drango, which was already connected to Kanze by a motor road. Work had started on this project when I fled to join the guerrillas.

By now the Chinese had established a large military base in Nyarong. Confronted with overwhelming numbers and superior arms, the guerrillas were slowly losing ground. Many Tibetans employed by the Chinese frequently exasperated their masters with their lack of co-operation and their sullen attitudes. Faced with almost daily defections of their "diligent ones," the Chinese now harboured a deep mistrust of all their Tibetan officials. Such people appointed by the Chinese were now frequently disappearing, many of them even stealing Chinese weapons and departing with them.

I heard news that the big guerrilla bases were now scattered into small bands, and I knew I had to leave soon and fight before it was too late.

9 Flight

The white crane is the bird of the north,
Born there ... yet he flies south.
The north is not an unhappy land,
But winter ice has gripped the blue lakes.

Folk song from Nyarong

On the eighteenth day of the eighth moon, 1958, I was granted a short holiday to vist my home. This provided me with a breathing space during which I would not be under the scrutiny of the Chinese. I decided to use this opportunity to join the guerrillas.

At first, I thought of leaving behind my wives and daughter, and proceeding alone. However, I changed my mind when I realised the Chinese would be sure to kill or imprison them in retaliation for my "defection." But even if I took them with me, they would inevitably be exposed to great dangers and hardships; yet they would have a chance, a slim one, undoubtedly, but at least a chance. And if we were to die, it would be better to die together as a family.

My brother Wangchen wanted to go with me. His wife had died earlier, but he brought along his young son. Another addition to our group was a close cousin of mine called Dowong, who had his only son with him. There was also my friend Kyau Apon with his wife and children. Three young men from our sub-district had confided to me their desire to join the guerrillas. These people were from poor families, and had been previously working for the Chinese. One of them, Sonam Rinzin, had even been a hsiang tang in our subdistrict.

124

These three men now came with us. With Nima, we were, in all, a party of sixteen.

Our preparations were badly disrupted when I received a letter from the Castle, ordering me to return for a special meeting. All of us gathered to discuss this new problem. We needed a few more days to collect rifles and ammunition (which we were very short of) from some distant friends. If I went to the Castle, times were so uncertain that I might never return. Yet if I did not attend the meeting, the Chinese would certainly suspect something. Finally we decided we would have to cut short our preparations, forget the spare rifles and ammunition, and depart that very night.

We left our home on the twenty-third night of the eighth moon. As we rode out in the dark, I prayed we would be able to return when times were better. It was a faint hope, but deep down inside I knew this was the last time I would ever see my home. All of us were silent, wrapped in our own thoughts and only the hollow clip-clop of the horses' hooves disturbed the night.

We were not a very formidable force. There were ten men and we had only four rifles between us: a Czech bolt-action with eighty rounds, an old Chinese rifle with twenty rounds, and a British Enfield with only five rounds. I also had my Russian rifle, but at the moment it was useless as I had no ammunition for it. It was not much to fight the Chinese with, yet I felt I had made the right decision, and that there was no use in being a man if I did not have the courage to rise and fight the enemy.

We rode throughout the night, and early next morning reached Zamdo, in Western Nyarong. The lower reaches of this land were occupied by nomads, while the higher areas were wild and rocky. We had heard of the existence of a large group of guerrillas based in this region and intended to contact them.

We had three mules to carry our provisions, and we discovered that in our haste we had overloaded them. So we cached three sacks of tsampa between some large rocks and tried to cover them as best as we could. We decided to ride up into the higher regions where we would be safer from Chinese patrols. We also split our force, and had some men ride ahead to scout. My cousin Dowong, Nima, and two of the young men (who had previously worked for the Chinese) were given this task. They were entrusted with two rifles and most of our ammunition. The rest of us proceeded slowly through the high hills. A few days later, we came to a large stretch of rocks. The whole hillside was littered with boulders and stones of every conceivable shape and size, and our progress was slowed down considerably. Most of us had to dismount and lead our horses through this maze of rocks.

Around noon, young Sonam Rinzin shouted to me and as I looked to where he was pointing, I saw a company of Chinese soldiers lower down the hill. They had already spotted us and were charging up with their rifles ready. The soldiers were only about six hundred paces away when Sonam Rinzin and I (only the two of us had rifles) ran down the hill to meet them. I rammed a cartridge into the breach and took a snap shot. A puff of dust rose before the nearest soldier, and a few of them quickly dropped down flat on the ground. I fired another round but didn't pause to see whether I had hit anyone. Sonam Rinzin was also firing and he killed a Chinese with his second shot. They hit one of our mules, which died instantly. Meanwhile the horses had panicked, and although Wangchen and the women tried to catch them, they did not succeed. But the women and children managed to scatter and ran away through the rocks. Only Sonam Rinzin and I were left. He fired a few more rounds and as I was preparing to do the same we discovered that some of the soldiers were trying to flank us. I had only three bullets left (I only had five to start with), so we retreated through the rocks, away from the spot from which the women and children had fled. The extreme rugged-ness of the terrain prevented the soldiers from pinning us down, and we managed to escape. The Chinese gave up the chase after about two hours and, collecting our scattered horses and supplies, we soon departed.

Around dusk, Sonam Rinzin and I headed for the lower reaches of the hill where we had previously hidden some supplies. I felt that the rest of the party (if they had managed to escape) would assemble there. We waited anxiously the whole night but no one came. Next morning, our scouting party showed up. We explained what had happened, and then four of us went up the hill to look for our missing members. We searched through that craggy morass of rocks and finally found my elder wife, my friend Kyau Apon and one servant. Although we kept up the search the whole day, we did not find anyone else. The next day we searched again, but it was only on the third day that we found, shivering beside some boulders, my younger wife and my little daughter, and Kyau Apon's wife and children. They had hidden behind the boulders for three nights, not daring to come out. They had had nothing to eat or drink during that time but were all surprisingly fit and none the worse for their fearful experience. Only Kyau Apon's daughter was a little sick, but she recovered after a few days.

We never found my brother Wangchen and his son.

When we tried to assess what we had left, we found that we had only one saddle and the one old blanket that my elder wife had taken with her when the fighting began. Of course, we still had the four horses of our scouting party, but we had no cooking pots. As for provisions, we had only the three sacks of tsampa we had hidden earlier. Some of us went down the valley and happened to meet a few villagers who gave us some supplies and a brass pot. After a few days we fortunately met a band of guerrillas from Upper Nyarong, amongst whom were two of my acquaintances, Gyari Dorjee Gyalsten and Rinchen Wangyal. Veterans of many battles against the Chinese, they were in search of ammunition and food to replenish their supplies. They had about thirty men in their band and also their families. They did not have many horses. Yet they shared what supplies they had with·us, and we decided to join them.

We learnt from these men that during the previous year, there had been a considerable guerrilla force, over 10,000 people, in Tromtha, a day's ride from Zamdo where we were. But due to Chinese pressure and the problems of supplying such a large force, they had split up. One of the biggest bands, under Gyari Nima, had headed for Lhasa in the fifth moon. Another group, under Ghaba Dorjee Gompo, had also departed for Lhasa around the same time. But the journey to Lhasa was a long one, and one had to fight through many Chinese patrols to get there. Some groups that had too many women, children and old people could not possibly accomplish the journey and had to stay behind. Such was the case with the bands of Thongcha Nima and Phise Ato. Yet they were still operating in western Nyarong and constantly raiding Chinese out-posts and patrols. In the forest of lower Zamdo I also met an old acquaintance, Dorjee Samdup, who had been a chief lieutenant of Gyari Nima. He was badly wounded and could not leave for Lhasa, but his three strapping sons and his small band still stood loyally by him.

There were many other such guerrilla bands scattered all over Nyarong. Too many of them were encumbered with women and children and did not have sufficient weapons and ammunition. Yet they persevered and refused to surrender. Two of the more famous bands were those under Tashi Wangyal (Gyari Nima's younger brother) and Ari, both having more than a hundred men each.

We stayed at Zamdo for some time and made plans to acquire more rifles, ammunition and also supplies. We left the women and children high up on the rocks, and proceeded down the valley to the nearby villages where we had friends. We managed to get supplies, although weapons proved to be a more difficult proposition. But we did get some ammunition from a Tibetan who was a local official under the Chinese. I also sent some men back home to contact my friends, and bring the ammunition we had to leave behind earlier.

Then, with our families, we rode off to another area nearby

called Trodha Nyoko. We still had great difficulties because of lack of horses, but we learnt there was a large Chinese camp in neighbouring Tromkhog, and they had plenty of horses. Leaving our families again, we rode off to raid the Chinese camp.

Our scouts discovered that the Chinese camp was down in a valley and had a constant garrison of five hundred soldiers. But they grazed their horses high up on the hills, a few miles away from the camp. We managed to get close to the large herd and spotted only about twenty guards. Cautiously we crept up undetected and let loose a hail of bullets. Every one of them fell down dead, and we were able to drive away seventy horses with us.

We headed back fast to Trodha Nyoko. As we rode around a bend in a narrow ravine we suddenly encountered eight mounted Chinese soldiers. All of us, including the soldiers, were taken by surprise. We stared at each other for a brief moment and just as we prepared to fight, one Chinese raised his hands in surrender. A few seconds later the rest of the soldiers nervously followed suit. Most of them were raw recruits having no battle experience and they begged us to spare their lives. Some young men in our band wanted to kill them, and one lad went so far as to break a soldiers arm with the blunt side of his sword. But the older men and I told them to stop and said it was a sinful thing to do. We stripped the soldiers of their horses, guns and clothes and sent them away, free and naked as the day they were born. The condition of our band had now greatly improved as we had spare horses and more guns than we had before. At this point we were about forty men and sixty women and children. Four of us older men led the band: there was Anor, Gyari Dorjee Gyalt-sen, Rinchen Wangyal and myself.

We proceeded north to Ase Ta Kham, (the "Horse land of Ase," Ase being a hero of our old legends). We had barely arrived there when our scouts reported the approach of fifty Chinese soldiers. We prepared an ambush and managed to kill five of them. The rest withdrew. But soon afterwards, we were attacked by about a hundred soldiers. While we held them off, our wives and children loaded the horses with our provisions and managed to get away. Finally we broke off the fight and made a fast retreat. The Chinese did not follow us. We killed about eight of them. On our side, two of the young men (the ones who had worked for the Chinese) were killed and we also lost Sonam Rinzin. We caught up with our women before dusk.

Towards the end of the tenth moon of 1958, Chinese pressure made itself felt. We knew we could do nothing in Nyarong and decided to head for Lhasa. We realised that the Chinese were there too, but what mattered was that our leader and guide, the Dalai Lama was also there. Many other guerrilla bands were heading in that direction as were refugees fleeing the savage reprisals and the now open brutalities of the Chinese.

We travelled past Derge Yhilung, and towards nightfall encountered another company of Chinese troops. We began firing at each other and finally the Chinese disengaged. Two of our men were killed. The Chinese suffered about twenty casualties. That same night we crossed the Zachu river. The Zachu is actually the same river that flows through Nyarong, the Nyakchu. But our people refer to the river north of Kanze as the Zachu; and when it flows south of that town it is known as the Nyakchu. East of Zachu are the grasslands of Zachukha, the home of a fierce nomad tribe of about three to four thousand families. At this time there were no Chinese in Zachukha. They were instead operating west of the river where they had built roads, and had many strong garrisons.

We crossed the Zachu river at Danang. As soon as we got across, we encountered sporadic rifle-fire. However, no one was hurt on our side. It was probably the bad light that saved us. After recovering from the initial shock, we counter-attacked. There were just a few soldiers and they put up only a slight resistance before they left. We then met some of the nomads of the region who informed us that though the eastern side of the river was in guerrilla hands, there were heavy concentrations of Chinese on the western side. We also learnt that the rebels had sent messages to the Tibetan Government in Lhasa, informing them of the situation, and had also tried to contact the "Four Rivers and the Six Ranges" resistance force, the biggest guerilla force of them all — operating in Lhoka, the district south of Lhasa.

The messengers were expected back at any time. We waited hopefully for several days, but they did not return, so we decided to raid a nearby Chinese base at Zamey Naghdo somewhat south of our encampment as our spies had reported that it had large supplies of food and equipment. We joined forces with the local guerrilla bands who were from the tribes of Bachu, Yadi and Thargyen. There was also a group of nomads from Zapa-Liru in Nyarong, and then there was our own smalll band. In all, we had a force of three hundred men for our raid. We expected the raid to be a pushover as our scouts reported that there were only twenty to thirty Chinese soldiers guarding the camp. But somehow news of our proposed raid must have leaked out, because when we got there we found about two hundred Chinese soldiers waiting for us. These soldiers were normally stationed at the Zokchen monastery, a few days ride away. It wasn't as easy as we had hoped, though casualties were not too heavy on either side. The Chinese wisely disengaged early and barricaded themselves in their camp. We managed to take the horses (about two hundred of them) and about eight hundred dres and yaks. Although it wasn't really a victory as we hadn't wiped out the garrison, the local people insisted on calling this incident the "the victory of the five tribes."

That day we lost one of our best fighters, a strapping young lad from Nyarong called Nolo. A Chinese bullet got him right in the middle of his forehead.

When the Chinese first came to Tibet, they constantly and vociferously declared that they not only respected but actively supported "freedom of religion." They patronised the lamas and leading religious figures, and even asserted that the Lord

Buddha was a "true proletariat hero" as he had renounced his royalty and wealth. Their change of attitude began with the initiation of "democratic reforms" in 1956. From then on, every party communique gradually increased in its opposition to the monasteries until they were finally totally hostile towards religion:

> ... Freedom of religion must be respected but monasteries must conclude all loan transactions with the people, and must not lend any more money ...

> ... People may pay back loans to the monasteries of their own free will; but the monasteries may not demand payment ...

> ... People must not pay back loans to monasteries. All loans will be settled by the People's Government ...

> ... The People's Government will not pay the monasteries for the past debts of the people. The monasteries are instead required to invest all their capital in local co-operative ventures ...

> ... Freedom of religion is only for individuals. No organisations may be created for religious reasons, nor may the monks proselytize ...

> ... All monks and priests must work. All monks performing *shabten* (ritual prayers) in households, must be paid wages, equivalent to that of a common labourer ...

> ... Religion is based on ignorance, and fed by blind faith ...

> ... 1958 ... Religion is the opium of the people. All monks and lamas are exploiters and enemies of the people. The Red [clergy] and Black [aristocracy] enemies must be exterminated.

Earlier I mentioned that the particular garrison we fought was normally stationed at the monastery of Zokchen. There were two famous monasteries about a day's ride from Zachukha, they were the Zokchen Gompa and the Shichen Gompa, both of the Nyingma order. These monasteries had a permanent congregation of about a thousand monks. The two monasteries, especially Zokchen, were famous throughout Tibet for the many saintly and learned lamas and ascetics they had produced.

The Chinese had come to the Zokchen monastery and demanded that the monks of the Zokchen and Shichen monasteries attend a special meeting. The Chinese had then proceeded to occupy the best quarters in the monastery, which was the residence and personal college of the chief lama, Zokchen Rinpoche. They kept the Zokchen Rinpoche and all other prominent lamas as hostages with them. At the meeting, the Chinese informed the assembled monks that henceforth all monks were to disrobe and marry. They also made the monks work, chopping trees in the neighbouring forest, and held constant criticism sessions and meetings for about two months. The sacred images of the Buddhas and other deities were torn down; the sacred books thrown onto the ground and the monks forced at gunpoint to walk on them. On the twenty-fifth day of the eighth moon in 1958, the Chinese announced that the monks would have to criticise their abbots and lamas in "struggle" session.

These "struggle" were diabolically cruel criticism meetings where children were made to accuse their parents of imaginary crimes; where farmers were made to denounce and beat up landlords; where pupils were made to degrade their teachers; where every shred of dignity in a person was torn to pieces by his people, his children and his loved ones. Old lamas were made to have sex with prostitutes in public. And often the accused was beaten, spat and urinated upon. Every act of degradation was heaped upon him — and it killed him in more ways than one. When someone was through in a thamzing session, no one ever spoke of him again. He was no martyr for the people, because the people had killed him. His death lay in the hands of those who should have honoured and remembered him; but in their guilt, the people tried to forget him and the shameful part they had played in his degradation.

The monks of Zokchen met secretly to discuss what they should do. One monk called Nyarong Gyulo, originally from my province, spoke out his intentions:

"We have witnessed terrible acts of sacrilege and blasphemy with much forbearance — some would say, with much cowardice. Now the Chinese want us to denounce our lamas, our very teachers who taught us the Dharma, who gave us the precious initiations and who passed the sacred teachings of Buddhism on to us. I know not what you all wish to do, but as for me, I will never denounce them. Let me die a thousand deaths and roast in a thousand hells before I ever contemplate such a terrible deed."

All the monks agreed heartily, and discussed what they should do. They decided that the only way was to fight. Before a senior monk, all of them gave up their monkhood to free themselves of their vow not to kill. Then they swore a sacred oath of secrecy and total commitment to the plan.

There were three hundred Chinese soldiers at the monastery and they were all well armed. The monks had nothing but swords, knives and the axes the Chinese had given them to cut trees. The soldiers and officers were all quartered at the *labrang*, the residence of Zokchen Rinpoche, who was still being held there, along with other lamas. The monks decided to attack when the soldiers were having lunch, since at that time they could be expected to be off guard. A smaller contingent of monks would hack their way through the building to where the lamas were held and rescue them. The monks then chose Nyarong Gyulo to lead them. The Chinese must have somehow stumbled upon what was happening, for the night before the attack they made ready to arrest Gyulo. But Gyulo in turn discovered what the Chinese were up to, and without wasting a moment summoned all the monks and attacked. They stormed the *labrang* building, cutting down the guards, and getting inside, began to hack away with their axes at anything that moved. It was dark in the building and there was a great deal of shouting and confusion. The Chinese soldiers panicked and started to shoot indiscriminately. It was a bloody and chaotic massacre.

But one aspect of the monks' original plan was still working. The picked contingent of monks, ignoring the melée, rushed up to the top of the building and, cutting down the guards, rescued the lamas. The Chinese Commander and a few of his officers were with the lamas, and they were hacked to pieces. In the fighting Zokchen Rinpoche was wounded by a flying axe. The monks quickly rushed their lamas out of the building and called off the attack. As soon as all the monks managed to come out, they piled dry faggots, hay and other flammable substances against the side of the building. Ignoring the firing of the Chinese within, the monks set fire to the place. The Chinese that had survived the axes and the swords were all burnt to death. There were no survivors. About fifty monks were killed and many more wounded but except for Zokchen Rinpoche, all the other lamas were unhurt. The monks also captured eighty rifles and other small arms in good condition. Then the whole monastery made ready to leave.

We were in Zachukha when they arrived — about seven hundred weary, travel-stained monks, trailing their wounded and old feeble monks. Moved by the sight of their pathetic condition, the local people and the guerrillas generously provided them with good butter, tsampa and meat. The wounded Zokchen Rinpoche and his entourage were housed at the small local monastery of Wongpo Gon. The great lama died of his wounds after three days.

The abbot of the Shichen monastery, a venerable old monk called Gongsha, gave a special initiation called the Mani Lung to all the people in the area. After this initiation, and at the behest of some devotees, he also initiated the people into the mysteries of the Sem Tri (guide for the mind), the most sacred

Tantric initiation of the Nyingma order. Normally people are only permitted this initiation after they have accomplished the five preliminaries — 100,000 recitations of the three Refuges, 100,000 recitations of the Prayer of Universal Compassion, etc. These taxing preliminaries usually discourage all but the most sincere of devotees, but the old abbot decided that the people needed this sacred rite in these terrible times, and he wisely dispensed with the normal requirements. Thus even in our misery we were granted this great teaching, and thereafter felt we would be able to die with less bitterness in our hearts.

By the third moon of 1959, the whole of Zachukha, lower and upper, was surrounded by a large Chinese force — more than twenty thousand soldiers. We knew we had to get out of this encirclement or perish. One night, the combined force of all the guerrilla bands in the area attacked the Chinese lines at upper Zachukha and broke through. But due to the constant pressure of Chinese patrols we were forced to ride east to Dha Khog, where we met a group of refugees under the leadership of an old lama, Dhalak Shatsa Tulku. The lama himself was old and crippled, and the people he led were extremely poor and ill-equipped. Only a few of them were young and had rifles. Although it would be a burden, we decided that this group would be safer travelling with us.

We decided to rest for some time at a nomad encampment called Dhatoe Pengin Ma. We had only settled for three days when we were spotted by a column of three hundred Chinese soldiers. In the ensuing battle, we killed about twenty five Chinese soldiers but lost four of our men and the mules carrying all the supplies of Shatsa Tulku.

Now we rode north towards Golok and Sethak. Our numbers had swelled and now we were about two hundred families. The terrain became increasingly rough and we had to make frequent stops to rest our tired mounts. On reaching a place called Asag Nang, we were confronted by about five hundred enemy soldiers. While we fought, our women and children fled. We managed to hold the Chinese soldiers for about six hours. In doing so we lost six of our men, but killed about fifty Chinese and also managed to collect all the arms and ammunition of the dead soldiers.

On reaching Sethak, we found that the people there were also in revolt against the Chinese. These people were led by Rinzin Thondup, the chieftain of the Sethak nomads, Batse, leader of the Wangche Piko nomads. Doma Kyap of Kongtse, and Gungda Nyakchu, a famous warrior of Eastern Tibet. They had planned to leave for Lhasa but had been forced to postpone their departure as they did not have enough horses. The people here were willing to pay ten silver dollars for a single bullet. We joined forces and decided we had to get to Lhasa. Our problem was breaking through the heavy Chinese lines on the west and the ever widening patrols that pushed us east.

On the fifth moon, we set out for Lhasa.

Our large and struggling cluster of horses, mules, yaks, men, women, children, monks, old men and women and wounded warriors, slowly proceeded through the wild and rugged land.

Towards noon one day a large force of soldiers was sighted on a nearby ridge. The Chinese attempted to head off our band, but the warrior Gungda Nyakchu, with twenty men, rushed to the pass on the ridge to stop them. They met the Chinese vanguard at the pass and exchanged fire. Then with swords and pistols Gungda Nyakchu charged at the Chinese soldiers and fierce hand-to-hand fighting took place. Twenty Chinese were killed. Gungda Nyakchu and three other men died. But this gave us the time to get away, and we rode out of the trap as fast as possible.

Several days later, an aeroplane flew over us dropping leaflets. Printed on these sheets were the words: "The Dalai Lama has been kidnapped by the reactionary rebel bandits. These bandits have also attempted to stage an uprising at Lhasa but it took us only three hours to crush it. All reactionary bandits must now surrender. If you do not surrender voluntarily, we shall destroy you."

Despite the generally disheartening tone of these words, we

were overjoyed to learn that our beloved leader, His Holiness the Dalai Lama, was safe and not in the clutches of the Chinese anymore.

We now divided our forces into two groups. This was necessary as our large numbers made us conspicuous and hindered mobility. We were also hearing disconcerting rumours that Red reinforcements were pouring into Sethak. Our original band, with the guerrillas of Zakchuka and Dha-lak Shatsa Tulku's followers, left Sethak on the eighteenth day of the fifth moon, in 1959. The other group, consisting of the various guerrilla bands of Sethak, was supposed to leave the next day but was forced to lie low because of unusually heavy presence of Chinese troops in the neighbouring areas.

Our group numbered around two thousand people. Only four hundred of us were armed, and of these, only a hundred had ammunition. I now carried an Enfield rifle with over a hundred rounds. We organized our band on a tighter basis for this long trip. A hundred men were to proceed ahead as an advance guard while the rest, with the women, children and old people, were to follow. At the rear we also posted a screen of about a hundred riders.

Our band was in no position to afford a confrontation with the Chinese. We were desperately short of ammunition and our ragged group would most probably fall apart and be massacred if the Chinese really fought us. So far the Chinese had only undertaken brief skirmishes against us, and they had always disengaged first. I think it was their plan to push all the various guerrilla units to the east, and when we were lumped together, wipe us out in one stroke. The one advantage we had was our superior marksmanship. Every one of us had been handling guns since we were boys, and could thus make each bullet meet its mark. Chinese soldiers were, on the whole, poor marksmen. Furthermore, the semi-automatic rifles they used did not have the range and accuracy of our single-shot, bolt action rifles.

Five days later, while riding through a valley, we were intercepted by a patrol of a hundred Chinese soldiers. They somehow managed to get both before and behind us. At the same time our advance guard was also confronted by another strong force of Chinese. We fought from noon till nightfall. Shooting our way through, we managed to join up with our advance guard and, thus stronger, pushed back the enemy. Two men were killed on the spot with four others badly wounded. About three hundred families were scattered in the fighting and many were lost. The Chinese lost about thirteen men that day.

Our numbers much reduced, but still awkwardly large, we continued our long and seemingly endless journey. Again we ran into another strong column of soldiers and in the subsequent fighting managed to kill twelve of them before they withdrew. After two days we encountered a small group of mounted soldiers whom we defeated. We shot about four of them and captured thirty horses.

This constant fighting began to get on our nerves, and everyone became unusually jumpy and uneasy. The actual fighting wasn't so bad; it was the breaks in between that kept us fearful and apprehensive, waiting for that inevitable cry "*Gya lay so!* The Chinese have come!"

After fighting another battle with the Chinese soldiers a few days later, we arrived at a place called Netoe. We spread a screen of riders to scout the surrounding areas, but in spite of this precaution a force of five hundred Chinese bypassed our scouts undetected and suddenly appeared on the ridge, within view of our camp. Caught unawares, we managed to make a disorderly retreat. We regrouped a little way further off and made a stand. But the Chinese had machine guns and shot down four of our men and wounded three before they finally withdrew.

We caught up with our women and children, who had fled ahead, and realized we had lost most of our saddles, cooking pots, and provisions. It was a minor disaster. We managed to catch only some of the horses that had stampeded during the fighting. For many days, all we ate was raw meat. We had no pots to cook anything, and all we had to drink was ice-water.

It was getting harder for all of us. My little daughter rode uncomplainingly with me on my horse. I held her frail little body close to me and a great bitterness gripped my heart.

The weather grew increasingly colder and fierce winds howled around our pathetic caravan. At the miserable and windswept plains of Go Mamo Sang, we came across a solitary nomad family who informed us that the entire land of Zachuka had fallen to the Chinese, and most of the guerrillas were either dead or had fled. We also learnt that a group of Chinese soldiers were encamped half a day's journey away, guarding the loot they had plundered from the people of upper Zachuka. We decided to attack this column and get some utensils, provisions and saddles. Twenty-five of our men, including my friend Nima, left immediately to scout, and we decided to meet them at a rendezvous about three day's ride from where the soldiers had their camp.

As we rode ahead we came across a nomad camp in the distance. Our hearts rose as we hoped we could get some provisions from them. But there was something strange and silent about this camp, and as we rode closer it became all too horribly apparent. We were greeted by a scene of total devastation. Blood stained and rotting corpses of men, women and children lay sprawled across the ground in grotesque and pathetic positions. The big tents were slashed to ribbons, and the rags fluttered wildly in the evening breeze. There must have been at least four hundred corpses. The big mastiffs the nomads usually kept were eating the decomposing bodies, and were now totally savage. We had to shoot two that attacked us. I saw a woman lying on the hard earth clutching a baby. Both of them were dead, and a dog was savagely tugging at the leg of the baby, but even in death the mother refused to give up her child. Words cannot describe all that I saw that day.

Completely shaken by this terrible sight, everyone was moved to tears, and our own problems seemed very insignificant and small. My little daughter was crying uncontrollably and she asked me between her sobs. "Father, why do our people have to suffer so much? We have given them our homes and all our possessions. Why do they still have to kill all these poor people"? I had no answer. I held her closer to me on my saddle and we rode on. I remembered what Colonel Len had said at Thankya, when the Chinese were conducting the "peaceful suppression of rebels" programme. His words came back to my mind "... We are to exterminate them all, even the women and children ... If you squash the nits, there will be no more lice."

On proceeding further we were pursued by about three hundred Chinese soldiers. We fled for some time but being unable to shake off our pursuers, had no choice but to turn and fight. The skirmish lasted for about two hours. Two of our men fell as well as two Chinese. The soldiers occupied the site where we were supposed to rendezvous with our scouting party of twenty-five men. But we figured it would do us no good hanging around this area, and we withdrew.

I never saw my boyhood friend Nima again. Three days later, we met a group of a hundred nomads from Golok in the north. The nomads were fleeing from the Chinese and did not possess any weapons. Shetsa Tulku happened to know their leader, so we camped together for a day and obtained some cooking utensils and saddles from them.

Just after sunrise, on the second day, we were attacked by about three hundred Chinese soldiers. We fought them off while our women and children loaded our scanty supplies on our horses. As we fled, a large aeroplane flew over us. We were not too conspicious as we were only men and horses, but the nomads with their herds must have been very clear targets from the plane. Sure enough the plane dropped a few bombs on the nomads and killed a large number of sheep and yaks. The plane circled five times and it made its runs very low. On its last run it raked the herds with machine-guns.

We rode throughout the day and as night fell, reached the newly constructed motor-road between Kyikudo and Sining. We rode for three more days and finally stopped to rest by the side of a wide valley from where we could see the two lakes called the Blue Lake and the White Lake (the Tsaring and Oring Nor). These lakes marked the fact that we had come very far north. If we went any further we would be in the province of Amdo. I knew we had to get west, but till now we had inevitably drifted north as the Chinese patrols tried to push us east. All of us were very tired and our horses nearly dead with exhaustion. We decided to camp for a few days and let the horses graze.

The valley was very wide and green with good grass. Towards the west, the land rose gradually in a gentle slope. It was very beautiful. Of the two lakes in the distance, one was a clear azure blue and the other as white as milk. The sun sank slowly, and becoming larger, turned flaming red; yet I could look straight at it without hurting my eyes.

Across the glowing horizon, the dark silhouette of a flock of Saurus cranes flew in V-formation, breaking the endless silence of the highlands with their evening calls ...

It was the fifteenth day of sixth moon, 1959.

10 The Last Battle

Somewhere in the small hours of the morning it became colder, and light flurries of snow began to fall. I shivered in my robes and pulled up the corner of the large tarpaulin sheet that served as a blanket for my whole family. In my halfsleep, I faintly remembered we had not posted any guards, but fatigue and drowsiness drove me back to sleep again.

I awoke to the sharp crackle of rifle-fire and the ugly staccato of machine guns. It had stopped snowing though it was still rather dark, and a heavy mist covered the entire valley. There was confusion everywhere. Shouts and screams, strangely muffled by the mist, mingled with the frantic whinnying of horses. The gun-fire grew increasingly heavy and bullets zipped past us with alarming frequency. Occasionally, the grunts and screams of people who were hit and the low groans of the wounded would filter through the mist. Strange ghostly figures drifted by, trying to catch a horse as it galloped away.

From the intensity of the gun-fire I realised that this was a major attack. I got up and, slinging my rifle over my shoulder, directed my wives and my little daughter over to the west. They ran ahead of me; I followed, tucking my boots under my arms, my bare feet crunching the thin layer of snow on the ground. We didn't even get time to tie our belts, and our robes hung loose around us, sometimes tripping us up as we ran. Further up the slope I saw the indistinct shape of two horses, and I shouted to my wives to catch them. But the horses had their tether-ropes entangled around a boulder. As my younger wife went to untie the ropes, she gave a little cry and fell down. I rushed over to her and saw that a bullet had gone through her left shoulder. Suddenly my little daughter cried out and I knew that she too had been hit. I rushed to her and opened her loose robe. The bullet had ploughed open the skin of her belly, and her intestines were beginning to fall out. I cut loose the two horses and helped my elder wife mount one. I lifted up my wounded younger wife on to the other and bade them ride away. I quickly put on my boots and, carrying my wounded daughter in my arms, proceeded up the slope.

Through the mist I could see the vague outlines of confused action. People rode by, or ran around frantically trying to get away from the hail of bullets. As I ran up, I looked at my daughter's wound. Although her stomach was torn open, her intestines, as far as I could see, were undamaged. It was a crazy thought to have in the middle of that hostile wilderness, but I thought how if I could get her to a good doctor, she would be alright.

She was sweating and groaning with pain, and she begged me to put her down. It was the movement that hurt her. I gently laid her on the ground, and tried to make her as comfortable as possible. In a weak voice she begged me to leave and save myself. I held her to me gently and kissed her. I guess it is karma to love one's offspring — even animals care for their young. As she lay dying, disembowelled, on that cold snow patched ground, I felt a terrible sadness in my heart, leaving me empty and forlorn.

A little way up the slope I saw a riderless mule and, leaving my daughter, I went to catch it. I had managed to grab its tether-rope when I caught sight of my younger wife. She had lost a lot of blood and fallen off her horse. I lifted her on the mule and, making her as secure as possible, whipped the mule away. "Aten! Aten! Help me." An old lady I knew from my village called desperately to me. She was trailing a horse with her, but since she was old she could not mount easily. I helped her onto the saddle and she rode away.

It was getting light but the mist still hung over the ground in dark drifting veils.

Through the murky fog, two figures stumbled towards me, my friends from Nyarong, Sonam Gompo and Anor. They came up to my side, panting, but no sooner had we met, than we heard the many thundering hoof-beats of Chinese cavalry galloping towards us. There was no cover in the meadow, so the three of us cocked our rifles and waited. The sharp crackle of gun-fire broke through the thundering roar of flying hooves and suddenly the first dark rider burst through the ragged mist.

We opened fire and a soldier fell, his horse whinnying and rolling over as it too died. We kept up a furious fire, and soon the ground before us became a tangled mass of dying horses and men. The Chinese were firing from horse-back and their muzzle-flashes sporadically lit up the fog in fantastic and eerie glows. Most of the riders galloped past us and vanished into the darkness. In the fighting I was separated from my two friends and I retreated up the slope alone. I found my younger wife again. The mule had thrown her off, and she was in a bad way. I stayed near her and held her hands, comforting her. She begged me to leave, and took off her coral necklace and asked me to take it. But once again a detachment of riders galloped up the slope and I grabbed my rifle and ran down to meet them. A young lad from Derge Yhilung was shooting at the Chinese soldiers and I joined him. By now the light was getting better and we could clearly see the riders and their horses charging confusedly about.

We managed to hit about five of them. Suddenly, I felt a sharp twinge in my shoulder. Simultaneously, another bullet grazed my ribs, near my left armpit. I was separated from the young boy in this melée, and forced to retreat. I walked up the slope not really knowing or caring where I was going.

A little way ahead, and unconcerned by all the noise and fighting, a scrawny chestnut mare was calmly nibbling the grass of that lush meadow. I caught her and, grabbing the saddle, rested my spent body against her flank. The mist had completely dissipated and the sun had come up. In the distance were pockets of furious action that I could not clearly make out, but about a hundred Chinese riders galloped past me, about two hundred paces away. I managed to get on the saddle and was riding away when a bullet tore through my right calf. The pain was tremendous, but I grabbed the reins hard and urged the old mare onwards. After some time she began to falter and stumble despite all my desperate urgings and whipping. Finally she made one last valiant effort, struggling on a few more steps before falling down and dying. The bullet that had gone through my calf had also penetrated the mare's side.

Fortunately I found a shallow gully nearby and managed to hide myself behind its banks. I had lost a lot of blood and was feeling very weak and dizzy. A little stream ran through the gully and its cool refreshing water soon cleared up my fuzzy mind and restored some strength to my body.

Hoof beats! I looked cautiously over the bank. About fifteen Chinese soldiers rode past in a cloud of dust.

The wounds in my shoulder and sides were not so bad but the bullet hole in my right calf was extremely ugly. A large amount of skin and flesh had been torn away and I could easily put two fingers into the hole. I tried my best to bandage it with strips of cloth torn from my shirt.

I then lay back and tried to rest, but my thoughts were full of the loss of my beloved wives and daughter. To divert my mind I counted my bullets and found sixty left — I had used twenty. Looking over the bank, I saw a few dead horses, and knew if I was stuck here I would at least have some meat. I had no illusions as to the fate of most of our group. There must have been at least two thousand cavalrymen and they had managed to completely surprise us. The soldiers were the fierce *Hui Hui*, Chinese Muslim horsemen and formerly soldiers of the warlord, Ma Pu Fang, and were mounted on the sleek, powerful horses from the grasslands of Sining.

I lay there in the gully drowsing fitfully. Around noon I heard distant vocies and, looking over the bank, I saw a few soldiers going up the slope about three hundred paces away. I silently threw the safety catch of my rifle and waited.

Suddenly I heard footsteps close to my right, and quickly turned around. A Chinese officer was walking towards me. He had an automatic rifle slung around his shoulder and a Mauser pistol in his right hand, the lanyard around his neck. He was so close I could clearly see the little red star on his cap. He saw me and immediately fired two shots from his pistol. The bullets ploughed through the side of the bank, missing me. I fired, and he rolled over and sprawled dead on the ground.

The soldiers up the slope at once scattered. I hit one and also shot two of their horses. I looked around me and realised this was only a small patrol. Three of the soldiers were lying flat up the slope and I could not spot them clearly from the gully. Two of them had run to my left, behind a grassy knoll.

Suddenly, from the top of the knoll, a hand-grenade came arcing across the sky. It exploded some distance away, and as I was in the gully, it did me no harm. Two other grenades came spinning across in quick succession but did not get close enough. The fourth grenade must have had a longer fuse, as it rolled over slowly to the lip of the gully before exploding. For a moment, my world became a flash of yellow and red, and a dull roar followed the ear splitting crack. Except for the shock, I was not harmed, but I realised I could not stay in the gully indefinitely. I slowly crawled down the winding gully till I reached a spot where the bank touched the bottom of the hillock. I crept out of the gully and, crouching, ran up the side of the knoll.

A little way up I came behind a bluff, over which I could clearly see the Chinese soldiers lying flat on the meadow. I aimed carefully and squeezed the trigger. One of the soldiers jerked sideways and died. I threw back the bolt fast, and shot the other two in quick succession. I was anxious, as the other two on the top of the knoll would have heard the shots, and I ran up the slope as fast as my wounded leg would carry me. I saw one soldier busy doing something with his rifle. Only his upper torso was visible, but he did not see me. I shot him in the side of the head and he spun around and fell down. The other soldier was nowhere around.

Down by the slope where the three soldiers lay fallen, a beautiful white Sining stallion was casually grazing. I walked down the slope over to him. But one of the three soldiers was apparently not dead, for he got up and waving a Mauser automatic pistol, charged at me. He fired his pistol wildly as he ran, and only a single bullet came anywhere near me. I fired back and missed. I then knelt on one knee and aimed carefully and fired. He stumbled and fell. He got up again. I fired another shot that sent him sprawling for the second time. He was only wounded and he shouted to me: "*Ze bhu yu tha*! *Ze bhu yu tha*! Don't shoot! Don't shoot!" "*Nyi cha chao pu cho*?" I said in Chinese, "Will you give up your gun?"

He awkwardly pulled off the lanyard from around his neck and tossed the heavy pistol over to me. I picked up the Mauser and tucked it between my belt. In the distance I saw a rider galloping away — the missing Chinese on the knoll. I could have shot him — he was not too far — but all of a sudden I felt very tired and spent, and my wounds ached.

I picked up the automatic rifle from the dead Chinese officer, and with some difficulty, managed to get on the white stallion. I found a bag of dry steamed bread tied on the saddle, and I nibbled some as I rode away. I also found some coloured signal flags that I used to bandage my wounds.

That evening, I met a few of my friends and we continued our forlorn journey together. The next day we also encountered some more members of our original band, including the old lama, Dhalak Shetsa Tulku. Finally there were about one hundred and seventy of us survivors from our original group of about one thousand five hundred. Of our group from Nyarong, there was only my cousin Dowong, his son, and Anor.

Later on, by piecing together our various experiences and also hearing news from other people, we realised that nearly two hundred of our people had died in the attack and about three hundred had been taken prisoner. The rest had scattered in every direction. Most of our dead were the warriors who had tried to fight and hold back the soldiers while the women and children ran away. The Chinese had also suffered a few hundred casualties.

For the next ten days we survived on raw meat and pieces of ice that we sucked to quench our thirst. Exhausted, and in no fit condition for fighting, we reached the upper courses of the Machu river. There we encountered a large cavalry force of about a thousand men. The Chinese immediately gave chase and we fought a running battle, shooting down about thirty of them. Four of our men were killed but fortunately the rest of us managed to escape under the cover of darkness.

By now I was so weak I could not sit upright on my saddle and had to have someone constantly supporting me. My wounded leg was covered with pus and so swollen that I could not put on my boots. Without any medicine, not even proper bandages, I rode on. Two days later we managed to kill a yak, providing ourselves with fresh meat.

We were resting one night, dead tired, without even loosening our robes, when one of our companions from Zaba-Liru, Dabho, deserted us. He stole my beautiful Sining stallion and Dowong's mule, and also persuaded a few other men to flee with him. The worst part was that Dabho also took our guide, a nomad from that locality. So we stumbled on, haphazardly, in a general westerly direction. A few of us rode double, and weariness ate into our bones as the savage winds contested every foot of progress we made.

We reached a high rocky area by the side of a snow covered mountain and camped there for a while, letting our tired horses graze on the sparse grass. Suddenly we were attacked by a large cavalry force. The horses panicked, but luckily I managed to catch one. Some of us rode out as fast as possible, heading for the nearby pass. This time we were unable to shake off our pursuers, and while crossing the pass my horse was shot from under me. At the same moment I was also hit by a bullet in my right shoulder. I fell down on the ground, but managed to quickly crawl away and hide behind some boulders. My cousin Dowong had seen me fall and he quickly dismounted and followed me to the boulders. We lay there silently as the Chinese soldiers thundered past us after our group of riders.

My cousin and I found ourselves in a high and forbidding area, covered with patches of ice and hard snow. Just above us was a high jagged peak, covered with snow. We made our way even higher to the side of the mountain. It was extremely cold and windy there, but no Chinese would ever come this high, and we were safe for the moment. We rested under a low overhang, trying to get a little shelter from the wind. My leg had swollen very badly and was black and rotten with gangrene. I was constantly in the grip of a bad fever and totally delirious, and was sure that I was going to die. Dowong did his best to make me comfortable and although we did not have much to eat he made me suck pieces of ice and snow. After ten days, when my fever and delirum was at its worst, the swelling in my leg ruptured and a whole mess of vile stinking gangrene, blood, and rotting flesh came out of the wound. Every day after that large quantities of blood and pus trickled out. Dowong washed it with ice-water, and gradually it began to get better. Still there was a large hole, the size of a small fist, in my leg. My other wounds were clean and didn't bother me too much, only my right shoulder, which was very stiff. After our third day on the pass, Dowong went down to the place where we had camped (and where we had been ambushed). He found fifteen of our people dead, among them his fourteen year old son and Anor. He also found three lamas (belonging to our group) tied to the boulders. They had been whipped and beaten with rifle-butts until they died. We later learnt that Dhalak Shetsa Tulku had been captured.

There were herds of drongs in this inhospitable place, and the rocky slopes were littered with their bleached bones. My cousin managed to shoot one thus solving our food problem. As soon as my wounds healed a bit, we made our way westwards — towards the evening sun. I walked slowly, with Dowong supporting me, and we prayed constantly to the great Triple Gem and to the Dalai Lama. On the way we managed to shoot a gazelle that provided us with meat for some days.

Three days later, we met eight members of our old band. They had spare horses, and best of all they had cooking pots. Dowong and I drank many delicious bowls of hot water after that. We were now close to the highway that ran from Sining to Lhasa. In this wilderness there were the dried bones of drongs, and, oddly enough camels. It was an indication we were nearing Sinkiang, or Chinese Turkistan. We knew it would do no good to go to Lhasa so we moved further towards western Tibet, where the Chinese did not have many troops. Three days later we attacked and killed a group of twenty army surveyors and road workers.

We reached the upper courses of the Phantom river around the eighth moon, where we were reunited with the band of guerrillas under Drango Gungda that we had met earlier in the Golok-Sethak region. They were about two hundred strong and although they had faced many encounters with the Chinese were in much better condition than we were. We travelled with them to Amdo Mema, near Nakchuka. There we learnt that His Holiness the Dalai Lama had escaped to India, and also about the great uprising and the retreat of the Four Rivers Six Ranges guerrilla force to India.

The Four Rivers Six Ranges resistance force was started in 1958 at Drigu Thang in Lhoka, south of Lhasa. This movement was the direct offspring of the first and bloody revolt of 1956, which the Chinese only managed to control after a campaign of draconian reprisals and the indiscriminate bombings of many villages and monasteries. The movement consisted largely of guerrillas and refugees from Kham who had fled to Central Tibet after 1956. The swelling number of refuges and guerrillas in Lhasa, and their terrifying stories of thamzings, tortures, rape, executions and the destruction of religion, raised the emotions of revolt to a fever pitch.

A direct consequence of this was the great revolt of March,

1959, and His Holiness's flight. The Dalai Lama was conducted safely to India by the resistance fighters. It was their supreme task, for if His Holiness had failed to reach India, the Tibetan National Movement would surely have ended.

We decided to go to India, and picked a route through western Tibet and across the border to Nepal. When we got to Tsala Dzong, we again had a brief skirmish with a company of Chinese soldiers. One of our men was killed, but we got five of them.

In the twelfth moon of that year, we reached the nomad centre of Naktsang, where about a thousand men had collected to fight the Chinese. Their leader was a grizzled old nomad chief, determined to give the Chinese a rough time. The people there generously gave us ample provisions, and once again we had tsampa, butter and cheese to eat.

We had no further problems from then on, and we crossed the Jakpa la, or the Bandit pass, on the second moon of 1960, and entered Nepal.

The pass was cold and utterly barren, swept eternally by blasts of freezing winds. Patches of ice and snow dotted the rock-strewn and ravaged landscape, and not even a single blade of grass comforted this endless desolation. I leaned over on my hard saddle and the fierce angry winds clawed at my face and screamed and howled across the dark grey sky. Tears trickled from my inflamed eyes and rolled down my wind-cracked cheeks.

I will not bother my readers with any further accounts of my various experiences in exile.

Of the sixteen people who set out from my village, only four of us survived that long terrible journey ...

I pray for them: my child, my wives and my friends who died, and also for all those living back in my unhappy land.

That is all an old man can do now, pray. I request this boon of my readers, to join me in this prayer, so that the sufferings of my people may soon end, and the ancient nation of Tibet become free once again ...